SALTS OF SILVER, TONED WITH GOLD

The Harrison D. Horblit Collection

of Early Photography

CATALOGUE NO. 26.   Joseph Cundall. *Twenty Views in Gloucestershire*
(London: The Photographic Institution, 1854), pl. 14.

SALTS OF SILVER, TONED WITH GOLD

The Harrison D. Horblit Collection

of Early Photography

by

ANNE ANNINGER and JULIE MELLBY

edited by VICTORIA ALEXANDER

THE HOUGHTON LIBRARY

HARVARD UNIVERSITY

1999

Catalogue of an exhibition held at the Houghton Library,

March 10–May 26, 1999

Cover:
Studio of Giacomo Arena. *Group Portrait of the Arena and D'Alessandri Staff with Implements*, 1870 (catalogue no. 39)

ISBN 0-914630-22-9

Library of Congress Catalogue Number 98-075090

© 1999 The President and Fellows of Harvard College

Distributed by the University of Washington Press

TABLE OF CONTENTS

ACKNOWLEDGMENTS

The donation of the Harrison D. Horblit Collection of Early Photography to the Houghton Library is due to the generosity of Mrs. Jean Horblit, whose thoughtful placement of her husband's acquisitions at various institutions reflects the forethought with which her husband originally sought to preserve selected treasures. We applaud her decision to place the photography collection, in its entirety, at an academic institution where scholars from around the world will benefit from her husband's assemblage of nineteenth-century photography. We greatly appreciate her continuing support, not only for the books, daguerreotypes, prints, and cameras themselves, but also for a room to house them, for the cataloguing, exhibition, and development of a symposium to celebrate the opening of the collection to the public. Throughout the past several years, Jean has responded to our questions and requests with unending goodwill and friendship. Her energy and humor have sustained us, and we hold her friendship as the greatest acquisition of all.

The original champions of the Horblit collection's long trip from Ridgefield, Connecticut, to Cambridge, Massachusetts, were Anne Anninger, Philip Hofer Curator of Printing & Graphic Arts; Roger Stoddard, Chief Curator of Rare Books; and Richard Wendorf, former Librarian of the Houghton Library, now Director of the Boston Athenaeum. It is thanks to their energy, persistence, and acumen that the Houghton Library received one of the largest single donations in its history. We appreciate the ease with which Jeffrey Horrell, acting Librarian of the Houghton Library in 1997, joined our efforts. William Stoneman, current Librarian of the Houghton Library, has shown steadfast support toward the management and conservation of the collection.

The room that holds the Horblit collection was designed by Samuel Anderson, an architect whose vision and talent have given us a handsome space to match the collection's demands. A database to document the collection was planned and built with the expertise of Elaine Benfatto, Harvard University Library Webmaster, and we are grateful for the additional support provided by Kim Brookes, Assistant Director of Information Technology, Radcliffe College. Surveys of the collection that were completed before its arrival at Houghton were very helpful in our own cataloguing; we are indebted to Denise Bethel, Director of Photographs, Sotheby's New York, who identified and appraised the prints and photographically illustrated books, and to Clifford Krainik, who assessed the cased images, reference books, and cameras. It took three Houghton cataloguers to record this vast collection: Rachelle Dermer, Ph.D. candidate at Boston University, was of particular help with the initial development of the database; Stephen Pinson, Ph.D. candidate at Harvard University, examined more daguerreotypes than he ever imagined possible; and Laura Ellen Cochrane, M.L.S. candidate at Simmons College, saw us through to the end and was enormously helpful in the preparation of this catalogue. David Whitesell, rare book cataloguer at the Houghton Library, created detailed records for the books, albums, broadsides, manuscripts, and other printed ephemera in the collection.

Every member of the Houghton Library staff has, at one time or another, assisted with some aspect of the collection, from the processing of paperwork to building renovations, from unpacking to research for this catalogue. We relied on their scholarship and enthusiastic support, without which none of this would be possible. Special thanks are due to Brenda Breed, Curatorial Assistant to the Department of Printing & Graphic Arts, who lent her calm and thoughtful support to every aspect of this project. We are also indebted to the many interns, students, and volunteers who assisted with the processing of the collection, including Ellen Doon, Amy Driscoll, Abigail Fojas, Margaret Hale, Kelly Hoffman, Larry Hyman, Donald Matheson, and Samantha Rein.

The Harvard photographic community has joined forces over the past three years as never before, to share information and resources. It has been our good fortune to have been assisted by many Harvard colleagues, beginning with Deborah Martin Kao, Charles C. Cunningham, Sr., Associate Curator of Photographs, Harvard University Art Museums. We are grateful for her advice, in particular in developing a symposium to accompany the opening of the exhibition. A grant from the National Historical Publications and Records Commission, administered by Robin McElheny and Melissa Banta of the Harvard University Library Preservation Center, allowed for the survey and housing of all American daguerreotypes at Harvard, including over 3,000 cased images in the Horblit collection. We were fortunate to have Grant B. Romer, Director of Conservation and Museum Studies for the George Eastman House, help in prioritizing the goals we set for the initial processing of the collections. We are the grateful recipients of a Getty conservation grant that allowed us to undertake a study of the collection's paper negatives and photogenic drawing. This groundbreaking project was completed thanks to the scholarship of Lee Ann Daffner, Mellon fellow in the Department of Conservation, Museum of Modern Art. Our first of, we hope, many conservation interns was Dana Hemmenway, now photographic conservator with the Better Image, who worked on several albums of architectural photography. Conservators Nora Kennedy and Babette and Daniel Gehnrich initiated a survey of the collection's rare books and albums, which will be the focus of much future work. Studies in digital capture, led by Stephen Chapman, Preservation Librarian for Digital Projects, have helped us meet our goals for an on-line visual database that is accessible to the general public. As we go to press, we find ourselves the beneficiaries of a valued grant from the Harvard College Library Digital Initiatives Team, headed by John Howard, which will allow us to photograph and digitize 3,330 cased images in the collection. This project will provide complete visual access to the collection while preserving the originals.

Portions of the Horblit collection have been seen once before at Harvard, during the 1989 exhibition, "The Invention of Photography and Its Impact on Learning," and we benefited from the scholarly research of its curator, Eugenia Parry. We have also been fortunate, over the past two years, to share ideas with six eminent scholars: Hans P. Kraus, Jr., Grant B. Romer, Larry J. Schaaf, Robert Sobieszek, John Szarkowski, and Andrew Szegedy-Maszak. Their essays, published in a companion volume to this catalogue, *Six Exposures: Essays in Celebration of the Opening of the Harrison D. Horblit Collection of Early Photography*, have enhanced our understanding of the collection and paved the way for future scholarship. In addition, we appreciate the cooperation of Denise Bethel, Merry A. Foresta, Julia Van Haaften, Anne McCauley, Martha Sandweiss, and Alan Trachtenberg, who will help us celebrate the opening of the collection with a symposium.

We are grateful to all our colleagues and fellow enthusiasts who helped with our research of this vast collection. Time and again, our many questions were met with patience and insight. In particular, we wish to thank Paul Messier, Boston Art Conservation; Sally Pierce, Boston Athenaeum; Aaron Schmidt, Boston Public Library; Rod Hamilton, India Office Library at the British Library; Doug and Toddy Munson, Chicago Albumen Works; Mark Osterman, France Scully, Andy Eskins, Grant B. Romer, Joseph Struble, Rachel Stuhlman, and Roger Watson, George Eastman House; Julian Cox, J. Paul Getty Museum; Eric Holzenberg, the Grolier Club; John Huehnergard, Dr. Susan Miller, and Jeffrey Spurr, Harvard University; Mary Ison and Carol Johnson, Library of Congress; the Maine Historical Society; Joanne Lukitsh, Massachusetts College of Art; Chris Steele, Massachusetts Historical Society; Janis Ekdahl, Virginia Dodier, and Linda Serenson Colet, Museum of Modern Art; Thurman (Jack) Naylor; Kenneth Nelson; Michelle Delaney, National Museum of American History; the New Hampshire Historical Society; Sharon Frost, New York Public Library; X. Ted Barber, Parsons School of Design Archive; Sara Stevenson, Scottish National Portrait Gallery; Roger Taylor; and Mark Haworth-Booth, Victoria & Albert Museum.

We owe our thanks to Victoria Alexander, our editor and confidante, who read and reread our entries with never-ending patience, fresh eyes, and continued goodwill. For the design and production of this catalogue, we thank Duncan Todd and his staff at Champagne/Lafayette Communications Inc., who shaped both this volume and the companion book of essays. The photographers of the Widener Imaging Studio, Steven Sylvester and Robert Zinck, spent countless hours reproducing images from the collection so that each illustration might convey a true sense of the original. We are fortunate to work with such talented professionals and richer for their advice throughout this project. Photography for this catalogue was made possible by the Milton B. Glick Publication Fund. Special thanks to Lee Ann Daffner, Amy Rule, Laura Cochrane, and Maranne McDade Clay, who generously read the manuscript. The design of the exhibition was accomplished under the artistic eye of Bart Uchida, along with the lighting expertise of Stephen Buck.

Finally, we return to the Horblits, whose contribution to the Houghton Library has given Harvard and its visiting scholars a premier teaching collection on the history of nineteenth-century photography. Like Harrison Horblit, we have come to the study of photography relatively late but we intend to foster the exploration and study of this discipline with a passion equal to his. We offer this commitment, along with our thanks, to Harrison and Jean Horblit.

INTRODUCTION

At first glance, it might seem unusual for the Houghton Library, which recently marked the fiftieth anniversary of its founding, to be celebrating the gift of a foundation collection, but that is surely what the Harrison D. Horblit Collection of Early Photography is, even at this late date in the history of the Library. Harrison and Jean Horblit have been generous friends of the Houghton Library for almost as long as there has been a Houghton Library, and this latest gift is gratefully received in full recognition of their instrumental role in helping to establish the foundations of the Library's research collections.

Harrison Horblit served on the Harvard University Overseers' Committee to Visit the Library from 1949 to 1970, and he was Honorary Curator of the History of Science from 1963 until his death in 1988. In 1984 he established a book fund for the acquisition of "books about books, including bibliographies."

One of Harrison Horblit's first gifts to the Houghton Library, given in December 1948, was the 1470 edition of Pliny's *Historia naturalis*, printed by the first printers in Rome, Conrad Sweynheym and Arnold Pannartz. This volume was bound in the distinctive red morocco preferred by Thomas Herbert, the 8th Earl of Pembroke, and was too large to fit into the 1983 exhibition celebrating the fiftieth anniversary of Harrison's graduation from Harvard. The catalogue of that exhibition, *Collector's Choice: A Selection of Books and Manuscripts Given by Harrison D. Horblit to the Harvard College Library* (1983) does, however, include fifty-seven other gifts representative of many more manuscripts and books in fields that include early arithmetic, early English printing, the scientific Renaissance, printing and bibliography, bindings, and early photography. Pliny's encyclopedia of natural history is a cornerstone in the history of science. Less well known but equally fascinating is Cecco d'Ascoli's *L'Acerba*, a poem in Italian *sesta rima* that includes sections on astronomy and meteorology, stellar influences, animals and minerals, and, in its ninety-sixth chapter, a celebrated passage on the circulation of the blood. This fourteenth-century manuscript was formerly in the library of another great collector, Sir Thomas Phillipps; it was his MS 4573 and is now Houghton MS Lat. 290. Phillipps's name is frequently linked with that of Harrison Horblit, and we are therefore especially pleased that Harrison's gifts included Sir Thomas's set of the catalogues of the London bookseller Thomas Thorpe. In the margins of these catalogues Phillipps recorded his purchase notes and his private thoughts on the London book trade, giving today's scholars and collectors a special glimpse into an earlier era.

Sir Thomas Phillipps (1792–1872) is known as one of the greatest book collectors of the nineteenth century. He kept a personal library of approximately 50,000 manuscripts and an equal number of rare books at his house at Middle Hill, near Broadway, Worcestershire. Phillipps was also one of the first collectors and patrons of photography. His interest in photography began when he was looking for a method to document his manuscript and rare-book collection and grew into an appreciation for the medium itself.

In 1959, Harrison Horblit made one of his first purchases of Phillipps material. It came from the retired booksellers Philip and Lionel Robinson, whose firm, William H. Robinson, Ltd., had acquired the remains of the Phillipps library. This single acquisition brought Horblit 460 separate items, including books, tracts, leaflets, and broadsides printed at Phillipps's private press at Middle Hill. Horblit continued to pursue Phillipps material, and in 1961 the Robinsons offered him Phillipps's personal photography collection, which was still intact. At first, Horblit refused the offer, but happily for us, he changed his mind and on August 2, 1961, had the crate containing the collection shipped to his home in Connecticut. A typescript inventory prepared by the Robinsons survives. Sixty-three entries describe groups of daguerreotypes, calotypes and early prints, books of gem tintypes and *cartes de visite*, manuals, patents, and broadsides. One entry alone lists 420 photographs and 115 glass negatives. Early photographs by William Henry Fox Talbot, Joseph Cundall's *Twenty Views of Gloucestershire* (1854), James Robertson's *Interior of the Redan* (1855), and several Gustav Le Gray seascapes are among the many highlights.

Phillipps's photography collection was the cornerstone upon which Harrison Horblit built his own collection. Almost immediately after his purchase, he began adding to it, and the Phillipps material represents only a portion of what is now the Harrison D. Horblit Collection of Early Photography. Large groups of material, such as the Josephine Cobb daguerreotype collection and the nearly complete photographic estate of Giacomo Arena, were added, greatly expanding the scope of the collection. Today, the Horblit collection includes 3,141 daguerreotypes, 105 ambrotypes, 84 tintypes, 3,100 paper prints, 370 books illustrated with early photographs and photography albums, 3 cameras, and much more. An extensive reference collection of contemporary books and serials focusing on nineteenth-century photography complements the vintage photographs.

Early photography is not new to the Houghton Library, although its prior holdings cannot compare with the incredible breadth and depth of the Horblit collection. Important photographic material may be found in the literary and historical archives, such as portraits and family groups in the Henry and William James and the Oliver Wendell Holmes collections and more than 2,000 Civil War photographs in the Military Order of the Loyal Legion Collection. The Harvard Theatre Collection includes portraits of actors, views of theatrical performances, and both daguerreotypes and prints, by the likes of Mathew Brady, Nadar, and Napoleon Sarony. Many printed books with original photographs can be found in the Houghton stacks, among them Talbot's *Sun Pictures in Scotland* (1845) and Julia Margaret Cameron's *Illustrations to Tennyson's Idylls of the King and Other Poems* (1875), along with works by Charles Marville, Peter Henry Emerson, Edward S. Curtis, and Alvin Langdon Coburn. Indeed, across the Harvard University campus, in museums and libraries, photographic holdings document the early development of the medium and aspects of historical, literary, ethnographic, and social significance. The Horblit collection arrives at a time of tremendous excitement about the role of photography at Harvard and its relevance to the curriculum, with considerable energy devoted to its housing, conservation, as well as plans for shared access to digitized images within and beyond the boundaries of the campus.

Jean Horblit has continued the tradition of generosity established by her late husband. In 1990 she established a Houghton Library book fund in memory of Harrison D. Horblit for the acquisition of "rare books on the history of science." In 1992, in honor of the fiftieth anniversary of the founding of the Houghton Library, she donated Sir Thomas Phillipps's copy of Henry Fox Talbot's *The Pencil of Nature* (1844). This Horblit exhibition catalogue and the book of essays that accompanies it, *Six Exposures: Essays in Celebration of the Opening of the Harrison D. Horblit Collection of Early Photography*, celebrate a recent gift but also commemorate over fifty years of generosity by Harrison and Jean Horblit. Their gifts have provided a solid foundation for research by the generations of students and scholars who will visit the Houghton Library in years to come.

WILLIAM P. STONEMAN
Librarian

CATALOGUE NO. 5b.   American School. *Portrait of a Seated Man Holding a Walking Stick.* Half plate
daguerreotype, in gilt mat and carved wood frame with thermoplastic grotesque appliqués on gold criblé
ground.

CASE 1

Louis Jacques Mandé Daguerre

It should come as no surprise that the Harrison D. Horblit collection, which is devoted to the first century of photography, gives a place of honor to the discovery and early practice of the photographic medium and, in particular, to Louis Jacques Mandé Daguerre and his daguerreotype process. As a historian of science, Harrison D. Horblit was particularly interested in the journal accounts and manuals published, both in France and abroad, during the first decade that followed the invention. Included in the collection are the first published announcement of the daguerreotype in *Comptes rendus hebdomadaires des séances de l'Académie des Sciences* (IX, 1839, 250–67); the first two French editions and the first English editions of Daguerre's own instruction manual, *Historique et description des procédés du Daguerréotype et du Diorama* (all published in 1839); and two editions of Robert Hunt's *Manual of Photography* (both dated 1853). These serve as historical background to the more than 3,100 daguerreotypes, for the most part American, that Horblit collected over a period of two decades.

The riches of the Horblit collection, presented by Jean Horblit to the Houghton Library in 1996 in memory of her husband, are complemented by strong holdings in the Harvard College Library. Early nineteenth-century French stage designs and dioramas in the Harvard Theatre Collection document the fashion of illusionistic rendering and the climate in which Daguerre's early work would lead to photographic experimentation. Lithographically illustrated books in the collection of the Department of Printing & Graphic Arts at the Houghton Library, such as the Comte de Forbin's *Voyage dans le Levant* (1819), and the first volume of *Voyages pittoresques et romantiques dans l'ancienne France, Ancienne Normandie* (1829), by Charles Nodier, Baron Taylor, and Alphonse de Cailleux, exemplify Daguerre's early topographical work and his use of the camera obscura to prepare for lithographic illustrations. In addition, there are numerous copies of early photographic manuals on Harvard's shelves—manuscripts and printed works, European and American. Altogether, the Horblit gift and the university's other holdings constitute a significant research collection on the incunabula period of photography.

Louis Jacques Mandé Daguerre, 1787–1851

Historique et description des procédés du Daguerréotype et du Diorama . . . ornés du portrait de l'auteur, et augmentés des notes et d'observations par MM. Lerebours et Susse frères

Paris: Susse Frères and Lerebours, 1839
First edition, seventh issue; volume: 21 x 13.5 cm.

On display: title page and facing lithographic portrait of Daguerre by F. Jules Collignon

In the early 1820s, Daguerre, the darling of Paris, famous for his spectacular stage designs and fantastic illusionistic displays, began experimenting in secret with the idea of capturing permanent images of nature through the action of light. By late 1829, he was collaborating with Nicéphore Niépce, an amateur scientist who had been engaged for some time in a similar pursuit, capturing an image on a silvered copper plate rendered sensitive to light by subjecting it to iodine vapor. In the spring of 1835, Daguerre discovered that vapor of mercury developed the latent image. He believed that the method he had achieved for fixing the image was truly his own, and in 1838, after renegotiating his contract with Isidore Niépce, son of his late partner, he was ready to release the daguerreotype process to the public. He would have liked to have sold his invention by subscription, but failed to do so. He presented it to a number of interested scientists, academics, and politicians, including François Dominique Arago, astronomer, physicist, and member of the Chambre des Députés. Arago devised the scheme of having the French government acquire the invention for the benefit of all by granting a pension to Daguerre and Isidore Niépce. Arago first announced the invention at the January 3, 1839, meeting of the Académie des Sciences. By early summer, the bill granting pensions to the inventors had passed both Houses and, on August 19, 1839, Arago introduced the process at a joint meeting of the Académie des Sciences and the Académie des Beaux-Arts, held at the Institut de France.

At the meeting, Arago described the daguerreotype process but did not provide a step-by-step demonstration. The admiring but bewildered

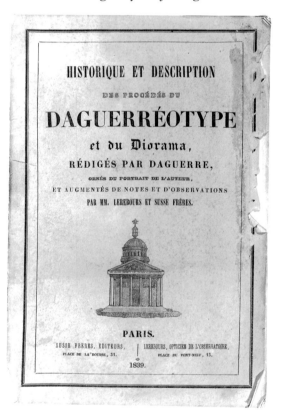

CATALOGUE NO. I. Cover of Louis Jacques Mandé Daguerre's *Historique et description des procédés du Daguerréotype et du Diorama* (Paris: Susse Frères and Lerebours, 1839). Volume: 21 x 13.5 cm.

audience was left to guess how to achieve similar results. An article in the September 10, 1839, issue of *Le Charivari* quipped that the art of the daguerreotype could be mastered by ordinary amateurs only with the assistance "de trois chimistes, de deux mécaniciens et de quatre savants divers, assistés eux-mêmes par l'inventeur" (Newall, 1953, p. 210).* To remedy this situation, Daguerre decided to publish his own explanation. His *Historique et description des procédés du Daguerréotype*, first published in September 1839, quickly sold out. Seven issues of the first edition were published in rapid succession, and a second edition was released the same year.

The Horblit collection includes an example of the seventh issue of the *Historique* and the first English edition of Daguerre's work. In addition, the Harvard holdings include two copies of the second issue, a rare copy of the fourth, and three additional copies of the seventh.

2

The Mechanics' Magazine, Museum, Journal, and Gazette, XXXI, no. 817–42 (April 6– September 28, 1839)
London: For the Proprietor by W. A. Robertson, 1839
Volume: 14.5 x 22.5 cm.

On display: No. 839 (September 7, 1839), pp. 424–25, "M. Daguerre's Photogenic Process," by Benjamin Cheverton

Founded in 1823, *The Mechanics' Magazine* soon became the leading periodical on industrial arts in England. The 1839 issues are of particular interest as they record for us the birth of photography and, in particular, the announcement and reception of the daguerreotype process in England. Within a few weeks of Arago's presentation at the August 19 meeting of both the Académies des Sciences and des Beaux-Arts, *The Mechanics' Magazine* presented its readers with a detailed account of the event and an evaluation of the process in its September 7 issue. A column entitled "The Daguerre Secret," excerpted from the *Literary Magazine*, described the session as a kind of "scientific *emeute*." According to this account, all the seats were already occupied several hours before the meeting was to begin, and more than 200 persons were turned away. As the meeting proceeded, "the most enthusiastic cheers responded from the grave benches even of the Academy, on the termination of M. Arago's description; and the President, M. Chevreuil, complimented M. Daguerre in the warmest terms" (p. 427).

Benjamin Cheverton's column on "M. Daguerre's Photogenic Process" was more reserved, however. Cheverton expressed disappointment at the "fragile nature of the effects produced," particularly since claims that Daguerre "had discovered some black substance, extremely sensitive to solar light in reference to its blacking power" had raised such expectations. It appeared, continued Cheverton, that the "process is essentially the same as that which Wedgewood, Talbot, and others have practiced in this country, namely, by submitting a preparation of silver to the *blackening* effect of light. . . ." Mr. Faraday was even said to have discovered a process quite similar to that of Daguerre, "which he nobly resolved to withhold from the public until M. Daguerre obtained his expected reward."

---

*Throughout the catalogue, citations in parentheses refer to the Bibliography.

In all fairness to Cheverton, it may well have been difficult to appreciate the innovative nature of Daguerre's process, since Arago had not actually demonstrated it at the meeting. Similar claims of precedence, in particular those made by Talbot in the winter months of 1839, had caused Daguerre in the meantime to patent his invention in England, a few days before "giving . . . [it] away to the world."

3

The Magazine of Science, and School of Arts, Intended to Illustrate the Most Useful, Novel, and Interesting Parts of Natural History and Experimental Philosophy, vol. 9.
London: W. Brittain, 1847
Volume: 25.3 x 16 cm.

On display: pp. 128–129, "On Photography," by Robert Hunt, Esq. No. V. Daguerreotype

Robert Hunt was born in 1807, the son of a ship's carpenter in the Royal Navy. Through a series of apprenticeships, Hunt succeeded in establishing himself as a druggist in his native city of Devonport. A brilliant chemist, he conducted experiments in his spare time, particularly in the field of photography from its beginnings in 1839. Throughout the 1840s, Hunt carried on an active correspondence about his photographic findings with Sir John Herschel, the astronomer and physicist, who was a close friend of William Henry Fox Talbot.

Arago's announcement of the daguerreotype in January 1839 caused a stir in England but revealed little of the process itself. During the next few months, Talbot's rival pronouncements and publications stimulated early efforts in England with paper processes. Robert Hunt immediately set to work, experimenting with photogenic papers and improving upon them by inventing and manufacturing the first direct positive paper. He kept abreast of French developments as well, and as soon as Daguerre's process became better known, in the summer of 1839, Hunt turned to experiments with the daguerreotype. By mid-April 1840, he had fully duplicated Daguerre's efforts and even perfected a daguerreotype process on paper of his own invention.

Today, Hunt is best remembered as the author of the first general manual on photography in the English language. *A Popular Treatise on the Art of Photography Including Daguerréotype and All the New Methods of Producing Pictures by the Chemical Agency of Light*, first published in 1841, not only records but evaluates early photographic processes. Hunt's writings did much to make the technique of the daguerreotype accessible in England and in America. Henry Hunt Snelling (no relation) acknowledged his debt to Robert Hunt as he generously paraphrased him in *The History and Practice of the Art of Photography*, published in New York in 1849. In 1851, Samuel D. Humphrey published the first American edition of Hunt's *Treatise*, advertising and reviewing it in his newly founded *The Daguerreian Journal* in the following words: "This work . . . has a more comprehensive view of our science than any publication hitherto upon the American catalogue. The Daguerreian operator will here find a very complete statement of the past and present position of the Daguerreotype art, together with all improvements both in Europe and America up to the present date (Hunt 1973, p. xxv)."

4
Thomas Winn

Directions in the Daguerreotype Process. A Direct Transcription of an Handwritten Notebook of 1846

Los Angeles, 1940
Unpublished typescript; illustrations include 22 albumen prints pasted in, and an original sixth plate daguerreotype inserted in the front cover; volume: 22.5 x 14.5 cm.

On display: cover

The compiler of this little volume was Albert Raborn Phillips, Jr., of Los Angeles, a collector of early photographs. It contains his transcription, typed in 1940, of an original manuscript dated 1846 that described in great detail how to make a daguerreotype. In the late 1930s, Phillips became interested in Abel Fletcher, a photographer active in Ohio in the 1850s and 1860s. Possibly through Fletcher's daughter, Lillian M. Fletcher, who was still alive and living in Los Angeles in 1940, Phillips became aware of examples of her father's work, both in the National Museum in Washington, D.C., and in the Los Angeles Museum. Some of his photographs can also be found in the Massillon Museum, in Massillon, Ohio.

Among the Fletcher holdings in the Los Angeles Museum, Phillips found a small red leather notebook, no larger than the palm of one's hand. It bore the inscription, "Presented to Abel Fletcher by his friend Thomas Winn, Richmond Va, 1846," and contained 72 pages on which, in a neat handwriting, Winn—of whom little is known—described his knowledge of and experiments with the daguerreotype process. Winn's chapters were well organized and explained, among other things, how to clean the plates and prepare buffs for polishing, mix quickstuff (a compound containing bromide, which

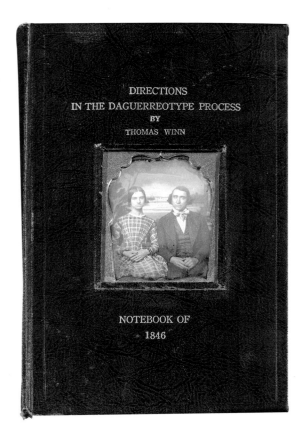

CATALOGUE NO. 4.   Cover of Thomas Winn's *Directions in the Daguerreotype Process. A Direct Transcription of an Handwritten Notebook of 1846* (Los Angeles: Unpublished typescript, 1940).

reduced the exposure time in the camera), coat the plates, and prepare hyposulphate and gild-ing solution as well as silver plate.

Phillips appreciated Winn's manuscript from the standpoint of the practitioner—he and fellow amateur C. H. Tremear, photographer at Henry Ford's Museum and Greenfield Village in Dearborn, Michigan, and Gladys Müller, photographer at the Franklin Institute in Philadelphia, were participants in the revival of the daguerreotype in the 1930s and 1940s. But most of all, as his introduction to the typescript makes clear, Phillips valued the notebook as a historical document. He saw it as a reflection of the extraordinary spread of the daguerreotype process in America after its announcement in New York in September 1839. He describes how, within months, all major American cities boasted studios of their own, and within a few years, every small town in the country had been exposed to the "new art," thanks to the work of itinerant daguerreotypists. Phillips lavished great care on this little volume, illustrating it with photographs of daguerreotype equipment, adding at the end a section entitled "Daguerreotypes Show at the Metropolitan Museum of Art, 1939," and having it bound in blue cloth stamped in gold, with the sixth plate daguerreotype of a seated couple inserted in the front cover.

5a

American School

Portrait of a Man, a Woman, Two Girls, and a Boy
Whole plate daguerreotype, in gilt wood mat; 25.8 x 20.7 cm.

For all their interest, the historic announcements, early printed reports, and photographic manuals in the Horblit collection would be less significant if they were not accompanied by the daguerreotypes themselves. The more than 3,100 daguerreotypes amassed by Harrison Horblit, most of them American, offer an outstanding historical representation of the process. The widest possible range in size, from mammoth to sixteenth plate, and presentation, from the simplest leather case to the most elaborate jewelry mount, is represented in the collection. The sheer number of images speaks to the commercial viability and popular success of the process, the fact that everyone, well born or working class, young or old, wished to have his or her likeness or that of a loved one captured for posterity. Though the collection includes outstanding examples from well-known photographers and studios—Samuel Bemis, Antoine Claudet, John Plumbe, Jr., Jeremiah Gurney, and Southworth and Hawes among others—most of the daguerreotypes are the work of unknown practitioners who photographed unidentified sitters. It is precisely this extraordinary range of images that fascinated Horblit. His "compulsion to hold onto as many nineteenth-century faces as possible" is the object of a full-length study by Grant B. Romer. Entitled "The Regard of Mundane Miracles," it may be found in *Six Exposures: Essays in Celebration of the Opening of the Harrison D. Horblit Collection of Early Photography*, the compan-ion volume to this exhibition catalogue.

CATALOGUE NO. 5C.   American School. *Portrait of a Seated Man.* Whole plate daguerreotype

5b

American School

Portrait of a Seated Man Holding a Walking Stick

Half plate daguerreotype, in gilt mat and carved wood frame with thermoplastic grotesque appliqués on gold criblé ground; 22.9 x 19 cm.

5c

American School

Portrait of a Seated Man

Whole plate daguerreotype, in oval passe-partout mat and carved wood frame; 34.7 x 30.5 cm.

5d

Daguerreotype case, leaves and flowers motif

Half plate size; leather and papier-mâché with mother-of-pearl inlay and hand painting; case (closed): 15.5 x 12.3 cm.

5e

Daguerreotype case, leaves and flowers motif

Ninth plate size; leather and papier-mâché with mother-of-pearl inlay and hand painting; case (closed): 7.2 x 7.2 x 6.2 cm.

CASE 2

William Henry Fox Talbot

William Henry Fox Talbot was a gentleman, a scientist, and an inventor. His accomplishments have been well documented, and his preeminence as one of the inventors of photography is secure. He is credited with many discoveries: photogenic drawing, the Talbotype or calotype, the use of a negative to create a positive image (positive/negative photography), early systems of photoengraving and photomechanical reproduction, and numerous modifications of photographic processes. Talbot attracted both strong admiration and intense criticism in his work, but has forever altered visual history with his invention.

Harrison D. Horblit was also a gentleman and a scientist. He appreciated Talbot's work not only for its aesthetic appeal, but also for the technological brilliance and ingenuity behind it. Horblit gathered the relics of Talbot's life and work, collecting information on patents and formulas as well as the photographs themselves. In all, Horblit acquired 172 photographs and engravings attributed to Talbot, multiple copies of Talbot's books *The Pencil of Nature* and *Sun Pictures in Scotland*, scrapbooks and magazines containing his photographs, along with journals of the period chronicling the development of Talbot's art. The Horblit collection allows us to see with Talbot's eyes, listen to his words, and contemplate the weight of his achievements.

6a

John Moffat, 1819–1894
Portrait of William Henry Fox Talbot
Edinburgh, May 1864
Carte de visite; 10.6 x 6.2 cm.

6b

John Moffat, 1819–1894
Portrait of William Henry Fox Talbot
Edinburgh, May 1864
Carte de visite; 10.6 x 6.2 cm.

6c

John Moffat, 1819–1894

Portrait of William Henry Fox Talbot

Heliogravure by P. Dujardin from a negative by John Moffat, printed by Imprimerie Charles Chardon aîné, and published as a supplement to the *Photographic News*, March 11, 1881; image: 12.5 x 9.5 cm., mount: 27.5 x 19.4 cm.

Some of the most important portraits of Henry Talbot are the result of a meeting he attended in March 1864 at the Photographic Society of Scotland. Talbot had come to hear "On the Light of Magnesium Wire in Combustion, as a Photographic Agent," by his friend and the society's president, Sir David Brewster. Later that evening, John Moffat, a prominent Scottish photographer and longtime member of the society, demonstrated Brewster's theory of "the flash." He succeeded in capturing two photographs, one of Brewster alone and the other with Talbot. Moffat later wrote to Talbot requesting a second sitting, and in May, Talbot was again photographed by Moffat at his Princes Street studio in Edinburgh.

The Horblit collection contains two of the views Moffat captured that morning in his studio. These photographs were published in the popular format of the day, the *carte de visite*. They are imprinted on the back with the seal of the Photographic Society of Scotland, Moffat's signature, and the advertisement, "The negative of this carte is preserved and can be reduced for the smallest locket or enlarged up to life size and finished in oil or water colors." The photographs came to the collection in an envelope with the handwritten note: "Portraits of H. Fox Talbot presented to the Society by CH Talbot esq., Lacock Abbey, Feb. 28th 1889."

7

The Mirror of Literature, Amusement, and Instruction

London: J. Limbird, vol. 33 (January 5–December 28, 1839)
Illustrations include wood engravings from photographs; volume: 21.5 x 15 cm.

On display: "Fac-simile of a photogenic drawing," cover of *The Mirror*, no. 945 (Saturday, April 20, 1839), p. 240

Talbot first read his paper, "Some Account of the Art of Photogenic Drawing," at the Royal Society of London on January 31, 1839, and abstracts were published the following month in *The Athenaeum*, *The Literary Gazette*, and *The Mechanics' Journal*, each without illustration. Numerous articles and letters about Talbot's discovery appeared that spring, but it was not until April that an attempt was made to illustrate the process.

d'après le cliché de John Moffat, Edinburgh

FOX TALBOT

1800–1877

Helio & Dujardin   Imp. Ch. Chardon ainé.

CATALOGUE NO. 6c.   John Moffat. *Portrait of William Henry Fox Talbot* from a supplement to the *Photographic News* (March 11, 1881). Heliogravure from a negative by Moffat; image: 12.5 x 9.5 cm., mount: 27.5 x 19.4 cm.

The Mirror
OF
LITERATURE, AMUSEMENT, AND INSTRUCTION.

No. 945.]   SATURDAY, APRIL 20, 1839.   [Price 2d.

FAC-SIMILE OF A PHOTOGENIC DRAWING.

Vol. XXXIII.   R

CATALOGUE NO. 7.   Golding Bird. "Fac-simile of a photogenic drawing" cover of *The Mirror of Literature, Amusement, and Instruction*, vol. 33, no. 945 (Saturday, April 20, 1839) p. 240; volume: 21.5 x 15 cm.

The April 1839 issue of *The Magazine of Natural History* carried an essay entitled "Observations on the Application of Heliographic or Photogenic Drawing to Botanical Purposes," by Dr. Golding Bird, a naturalist and amateur photographer. *The Mirror of Literature, Amusement, and Instruction*, a popular journal, then serialized Bird's text over six issues, beginning April 20, under the title, "A Treatise on Photogenic Drawing." On the cover of the April issue is the first facsimile of a photogenic drawing. This engraving was made by placing a branch of leaves on a sensitized block of basswood and exposing it to light, just as Talbot was doing with paper. The resulting photogenic drawing became the guide for the wood engraver, who would then cut the block and print from it.

Expressing his regret that Talbot had not yet published a chemical formula for photogenic drawings, Bird offered his own suggestions for preparing light-sensitive paper, capturing images, and fixing them "so that their otherwise evanescent character may not deprive them of their value." Talbot later chose the same type of leaf study to reproduce in *The Pencil of Nature*, along with a description quite similar to Bird's directions.

8

Commissioner of Patents

Patents for Inventions. Abridgements of Specifications Relating to Photography 1839–59
London: Great Seal Patent Office, 1861
Volume: 18.5 x 12.5 cm.

On display: Talbot's calotype patent, p. 5; dated A.D. 1841, February 8

This is the first of two volumes compiled by B. Woodcroft for the London Patent Office listing British patents related to photography. The second volume, covering the period from 1855 to 1866, was published in 1872 and includes items overlooked in the first. Although the first volume includes only brief entries for the 1830s, the complete text of subsequent patent applications is provided, including Talbot's 1841 application for a patent on his calotype process.

This patent, one of several Talbot obtained, became an obstacle to the commercial development of paper photography in England and was publicly contested a number of times, causing the entire British photographic community to take sides—chiefly against Talbot. The debate culminated in Talbot's lawsuit against Martin Laroche (née William Henry Sylvester), one of the many photographers in the early 1850s to use Frederick Scott Archer's new collodion-on-glass negative process. Talbot sued Laroche for patent infringement, claiming that the collodion process, which had not been patented by Archer, was just a variation of his calotype process and therefore covered under his original patent. Although the case was long and technically complex, the actual trial lasted only three days, and Laroche was found not guilty. In January 1855, exhausted and discouraged, Talbot allowed his 1841 patent to expire uncontested.

9a

William Henry Fox Talbot, 1800–1877

York Minster Seen from Lop Lane and Little Blake Street, 1845

Salted paper print from a paper negative; image: 16 x 20.2 cm., mount: 18.5 x 22.5 cm.

Many amateur photographers wished to meet Talbot and learn the secret of his successful photographs. One such enthusiast was his Welsh neighbor, Calvert Richard Jones, probably introduced to Talbot by their mutual friend and Talbot's cousin (by marriage), John Dillwyn Llewelyn. Jones was experimenting with many early photographic processes and often wrote to Talbot asking for advice, hoping for both a friend and a patron to buy his negatives. In the summer of 1845, Talbot sent Jones a copy of the fourth fascicle of *The Pencil of Nature* and suggested that they photograph together sometime. There was to be only one such meeting that summer, when Talbot, Jones, and Nicolaas Henneman (manager of the Reading Establishment, where *The Pencil of Nature* was being printed) took photographs together in York. Crowds gathered to watch these men each time they stopped to make a calotype. This print comes from one of only twelve successful negatives made that day. Both Talbot and Jones left the processing of their negatives to Henneman as well as the printing. Later that year, Jones took his camera with him to the Mediterranean but continued to send his negatives back to Henneman. Talbot eventually bought many of Jones's negatives to print and sell, leading to some confusion over the years as to the authorship of these photographs.

9b

William Henry Fox Talbot, 1800–1877

Loch Katrine, ca. 1840

Salted paper print from a paper negative; image: 17.1 x 21 cm., mount: 18.7 x 22.9 cm.

10a

The Art-Union, Monthly Journal of the Fine Arts

London: Palmer and Clayton, vol. 8, no. 91 (June 1, 1846)
Illustrations include one salted paper print from a paper negative; image: 16.5 x 20 cm., volume: 28.5 x 23.5 cm.

On display: Heriot's Hospital in Edinburgh, by Talbot, opposite p. 143

CATALOGUE NO. 9a. William Henry Fox Talbot. *York Minster Seen from Lop Lane and Little Blake Street*, 1845. Salted paper print from a paper negative; image: 16 x 20.2 cm., mount: 18.5 x 22.5 cm.

10b

The Art-Union, Monthly Journal of the Fine Arts
London: Palmer and Clayton, vol. 8, no. 91 (June 1, 1846)
Illustrations include one salted paper print from a paper negative (not shown); volume: 28.5 x 23.5 cm.

On display: "Sun Pictures or The Talbotype," by Royal Letters Patent, opposite p. 142

On February 15, 1839, editor Samuel Carter Hall launched a new magazine, *The Art-Union* (later called *The Art-Journal*). In less than ten years, the magazine's circulation grew from 700 to over 7,000, and it remained the leading voice in British art and culture through the turn of the century. *The Art-Union* chronicled the contemporary art world, regularly reviewing new books and exhibitions, and became a reliable source of information on the development of photography for the general public. Hall was an ardent supporter of photography, which he considered "one of the marvels—not to say miracles—of the age, the interest and value of which it would be impossible to exaggerate" (Hall, p. 3).

When the first fascicle of *The Pencil of Nature* was released in 1844, Hall published an enthusiastic review. Two years later, Talbot chose *The Art-Union* to further promote his work by arranging to have an original Talbotype inserted into each copy of the June 1 issue. Many different negatives were used to make these 7,000 prints, including some from *The Pencil of Nature* and *Sun Pictures in Scotland*. The Horblit collection contains twelve copies of this issue, with a different image in each: an ornate clock, a tower of Orleans Cathedral, a row of shops, a bust of a woman, a statue of a nude woman, le château de Chambord, two variations of articles of glass, a statue of the rape of a Sabine, a statue of a knight, Heriot's Hospital in Edinburgh (shown), and a cart and ladder beside a shed. Hall knew his magazine would benefit from the publicity generated by these photographs and devoted two pages to the promotion of Talbot's process over Daguerre's. "We presume," wrote an anonymous author, presumably Hall, "that the circulation of the very large number of examples with which Mr. Talbot has supplied us will have the effect of making many thousands acquainted with it who had previously only heard of it as one of the wonders of the age." Unfortunately, many of Talbot's prints faded, leading to public disappointment rather than enthusiasm.

Case 3

The Talbot Circle of British Photographers

Following Talbot's announcement of the photogenic drawing process and subsequent development of the calotype, a small group of friends and colleagues began to experiment with making paper negatives. Talbot not only maintained a legal hold over the calotype process but strove to promote himself as the leading authority on paper photography. The dedicated amateurs who endeavored to match his achievements would sometimes consult directly with Talbot. They also formed social networks to exchange ideas and images amongst themselves. Members of the Graphic Society, formed in 1833, began looking at photogenic drawings as soon as the process was announced and their interest led to the formation of the Calotype Society, or Photographic Club, in 1847. They were an organization, "composed of a dozen gentlemen amateurs associated together for the purpose of pursuing their experiments in this *art-science*" (*Athenaeum*, no. 1054, p. 1304). The club developed into the Photographic Society of London and, after 1894, into the Royal Photographic Society of Great Britain. Talbot's influence over these practitioners, inconsistent to begin with, gradually diminished until, in the early 1850s, the rapid developments in commercial photography left Talbot completely outside the circle of his own invention.

11

Nevil Story Maskelyne, 1823–1911

One Arch Bridge, Breconshire, 1850s

Salted paper print from a paper negative; 14.4 x 17.7 cm.

Nevil Story Maskelyne grew up at Basset Down, Wiltshire, about a twenty-minute carriage ride from Talbot's home at Lacock Abbey. The grandson and namesake of the Astronomer Royal, Maskelyne studied mathematics and chemistry at Oxford University, lectured in mineralogy, and became keeper of minerals at the British Museum. In 1840, a houseguest showed the seventeen-year-old Maskelyne how to make photogenic drawings. Soon he was experimenting on his own, converting his grandfather's camera obscura for his own use, and testing various mixtures of chemicals and papers. Maskelyne moved to London, where he became an active member of the Photographic Society and won Talbot's friendship after writing for advice about the calotype process. When Maskelyne's family complained that he was spending too much time and money on this hobby, he agreed to sell much of his equipment but wrote to his father, "My camera shall be my sole scientific companion, yet not a scientific one, I shall only make it an artistic one" (Morton, p. 52). Maskelyne married John Llewelyn's daughter, Thereza Dillwyn Llewelyn, who was herself a photographer, and together they continued to experiment with chemical formulas and photographic processes through the turn of the century.

The Horblit collection includes eight salted paper prints and one paper negative by Maskelyne. If you look closely at this pastoral scene, you will see the faint image of a man sitting on the rocks just under the bridge. This may be Maskelyne himself. The long exposure barely captures the still figure and rocks, while blurring the rapidly moving stream.

12

Views of Italy, Great Britain, and Elsewhere
Unpublished album of photographs by Calvert Richard Jones, George Bridges, John Dillwyn Llewelyn, and others, previously owned by Christopher (Kit) Talbot and his family, 1850s?
23 salted paper prints from paper negatives; volume: 31 x 25.7 cm.

On display: Two-Part Panoramic Study of Margam Hall with Figures, by Calvert Richard Jones, ca. 1845

As a young boy, Talbot spent all his holidays in South Wales, visiting his aunt, Lady Mary Fox-Strangways, and his cousins, Christopher (known as Kit) and Emma Talbot. Kit read mathematics at Oriel College, Oxford University, along with Calvert Jones, and later, Jones and his wife were often invited along on Kit's winter trips to the Mediterranean. Emma Talbot married John Llewelyn, and over the years, members of the Talbot, Jones, and Llewelyn families socialized together regularly at Margam Hall, Kit's mansion in Wales. They experimented with both the daguerreotype and calotype processes, often posing for each other on and around their estates.

The photograph on exhibit, attributed to Calvert Jones, shows members of the Talbot and Jones families posing at Margam Hall. A second Jones image from this album, depicting the Fourteen Stars Tavern on a street in Bristol, appears in the catalogue. The album also includes views of Pompeii, Cornwall, and Melbury Park (the birthplace of Henry Talbot). One image, titled *Desert Oasis*, is by George Bridges, another family friend and early photographer. Besides several family albums, there are thirty-two individual prints by Calvert Jones in the Horblit collection, and five other views of Margam Hall attributed to John Llewelyn.

13

Collection of Bound and Unbound Prints from Three Family Albums
Unpublished albums of photographs by John Dillwyn Llewelyn and others, previously owned by the Llewelyn family, 1850–1860s
Illustrations include 65 salted paper and albumen silver prints; volume: 56.5 x 38.5 cm.

On display: album page containing nine photographs of the Llewelyn family

CATALOGUE NO. 12. Calvert Richard Jones. *Fourteen Stars Tavern on a Street in Bristol* from *Views of Italy, Great Britain, and Elsewhere,* an unpublished album, ca. 1845. Salted paper print from paper negative; volume: 31 x 25.7 cm.

In 1833, John Dillwyn Llewelyn married Talbot's first cousin, Emma, thus assuring his place among the circle of friends and relatives experimenting with Talbot's new photographic processes. As early as 1839, Llewelyn was producing photogenic drawings, presumably having learned from Talbot himself. Although photography was never a commercial enterprise for Llewelyn, he experimented seriously with processes and chemistry, eagerly sharing his findings with Talbot and others. He was an active member of the Photographic Society of London, the Photographic Exchange Club, and the Amateur Photographic Association, publishing articles regularly during the 1850s.

The Llewelyn family albums in the Horblit collection contain photographs, lithographs, and original drawings of England and Wales, the south of France, and Crete. The album is open to portraits of family members. Horblit identified three of them as John Llewelyn, at the top; his wife, Emma Talbot Llewelyn, in the middle; and their son, William Mansel Llewelyn, at the bottom. The Llewelyns had four daughters, and the two pictured here are most likely Emma Charlotte and Lucy. Several drawings near the end of this album are signed "Charlotte Talbot" or simply "C. L. T." In addition to these albums, the Horblit collection contains forty-three individual prints attributed to Llewelyn.

14

The Journal of the Photographic Society of London Containing the Transactions of the Society and a General Record of Photographic Art and Science
Edited by Arthur Henfrey
London: Taylor and Francis, 1853–1854
Volume: 25 x 16.3 cm.

On display: Llewelyn's article on the calotype process, vol. 1, no. 16 (April 21, 1854), p. 194

The Photographic Society of London was established in 1853 by a small circle of enthusiasts for the "promotion of the art and science of photography, by the interchange of thought and experience among photographers" (vol. 1, no. 1, p. 1). The first public meeting was held January 20, 1853. After Henry Talbot declined, Sir Charles Eastlake was elected president, with Earl Somers, Sir William J. Newton, and Charles Wheatstone serving as vice-presidents, and twenty-one council members, including John Llewelyn, Calvert Jones, Nevil Maskelyne, and George Bridges. Their monthly journal contained papers presented at the group's public meetings or reprinted from other publications, letters to the editor, book reviews, and reports from other photographic societies. It was often used as a forum for questions, which were answered by the editors in the next issue, or to publicize newly discovered formulas or equipment. John Llewelyn was a regular contributor, beginning in 1854. In this paper, he recommends Talbot's original calotype process over the subsequent modifications made by other photographers.

15

John Pouncy, 1820–1894

Blaeu Point, the Seat of Mr. Brigstock, Co. Cardigan, 1859

Albumen silver print; image: 20.5 x 25.5 cm., mount: 22.6 x 29.1 cm.
From the collection of Sir Thomas Phillipps, title from Phillipps's handwritten note on verso

Sir Thomas Phillipps, along with Talbot, was one of the 100 subscribers to John Pouncy's *Dorsetshire Photographically Illustrated* (Bland & Long, 1857). In this publication, Pouncy advertises his Dorchester Photographic Institution and states that he "will, at all times, be most happy to take Views of any Places of interest in the County . . . and also Private Views of the House or Grounds of any Lady or Gentleman who may require them." It is quite possible that this advertisement caught Phillipps's eye and inspired him to document his properties. Phillipps commissioned 366 photographic views of his estate, as recorded in his *List of Middle Hill Photographs*, 1859. While 38 of these are described as "Mr. John Pouncy's negative photographs, September 1859," the Horblit collection contains 49 prints by or attributed to Pouncy, most with Phillipps's handwritten notes on the verso. These salted paper and albumen prints are primarily views of the houses of Middle Hill and the surrounding area, not unlike the views of Dorset that Pouncy had published earlier.

The Horblit collection contains Phillipps's own volumes of Pouncy's *Dorsetshire Photographically Illustrated*, which was the first English book illustrated with photolithographs. In addition, Phillipps saved a broadside announcing, "(For private use only, and not for publication) Pouncy's Process of Photographic Carbon-Printing," with Pouncy's notations in the margins. The broadside was printed in 1856, two years before Pouncy took out a patent on the process or publicly exhibited the work.

16

Robert Henry Cheney, 1800–1866

Photographs R. H. C.

Unpublished portfolio, ca. 1860
26 unbound albumen silver prints from Cheney's waxed-paper negatives, printed by Alfred Capel-Cure; image: 18.2 x 21.9 cm., volume: 27 x 32 cm.

On display: Dartmouth

Robert Henry Cheney was born into the privileged class, the son of General Robert Cheney of Badger Hall, Shropshire. After an extended stay in Italy, the younger Cheney returned to England, where he held such positions as sheriff of Shropshire and justice of the peace. He filled his time with artistic pursuits, including sketching, painting with watercolors, and writing art criticism for the *Quarterly Review* as well as a novel. Cheney began to practice photography in the 1840s, documenting favorite homes and local towns.

CATALOGUE NO. 15. John Pouncy. *Blaeu Point, the Seat of Mr. Brigstock, Co. Cardigan*, 1859. Albumen silver print; image: 20.5 x 25.5 cm., mount: 22.6 x 29.1 cm.

A fourteenth-century harbor city, Dartmouth was in decline during the nineteenth century, having lost much of its steamship business to Southampton. Cheney's photograph shows the Tudor House on Foss Street, with the medieval St. Saviour's Church in the background. Across the street is the birthplace of painter William Henley. The carved animal and human figures supporting the overhanging windows of the house are barely visible in the soft shadows of Cheney's paper negative. Foss Street is shown just before the city began an ambitious improvement scheme in the 1860s. For the first time in 500 years, many streets were widened, and houses on either side removed. The Tudor House withstood these improvements but was destroyed by bombs in 1943.

17
Robert Henry Cheney, 1800–1866
Photographs R. H. C.

Unpublished portfolio, ca. 1860
26 unbound albumen silver prints from Cheney's waxed-paper negatives, printed by Alfred Capel-Cure; image: 18.2 x 21.9 cm., volume: 27 x 32 cm.

On display: Holland House

Although Cheney's own photographs have not survived, prints made from his negatives by his nephew, Colonel Alfred Capel-Cure, can be found. One such collection of albumen prints is in the Horblit collection. Originally, it was part of a larger portfolio of prints passed down through the generations of the Capel-Cure and Stewart families. The largest portion of the photographs from this portfolio are now at the Centre Canadien d'Architecture in Montreal. The 26 remaining views were purchased by Mr. Horblit along with the front cover of the album, which bears the stamp, "Photographs R.H.C." On the back of this board is a penciled note, "The negatives of these Photos were taken by my uncle RHCheney on Paper between 1850–60, the Positives were printed by me, in 1859–60, <u>ACC</u>."

Holland House was one of the great houses of England. Built in the seventeenth century for Walter Cope, it was originally known as Cope Castle. Cope's son-in-law, the Earl of Holland, provided the house with its more enduring name. From the beginning, Holland House was the center of high society in London, frequented by a long list of distinguished guests, including Lord Byron, Sir Walter Scott, Charles Dickens, and several generations of the royal family. Robert Cheney's brother Edward was an inseparable friend of Henry Fox, the fourth and last Earl of Holland, and both Cheney brothers often dined at Holland House. After Fox's death, it was Edward who advised his widow, helping her settle her husband's estate and arrange the sale of their properties. Holland House was partially destroyed during the Second World War, but the remains can still be visited in Holland Park, off Kensington High Street in west London. The fifty-four acre park is only a small reminder of the great estate once maintained by the Earls of Holland.

CATALOGUE NO. 17.   Robert Henry Cheney. *Holland House* from *Photographs R.H.C.*, an unpublished album, ca. 1860. Albumen silver print from waxed paper negative; image: 18.2 x 21.9 cm., volume: 27 x 32 cm.

CASE 4

Photography and the Grand Tour: Egypt and the Middle East

Egypt and the Middle East fascinated the literary, artistic, and scientific minds of nineteenth-century Europe. From its very beginnings, photography played an essential role in the "Egyptomania" of the period, at once firing the imagination, recording archaeological and ethnographic evidence, and satisfying a deep longing for the exotic and the foreign.

The Horblit collection documents in a remarkable way the various roles played by photography on such travels: as a witness to the archaeological and literary expedition of Maxime Du Camp and Gustave Flaubert, for example; amateur pastime and means of recording the grand tour, as in the case of the young American and future architect Richard Morris Hunt; and archaeological and ethnographic evidence for the general public, as in the commercial enterprises of Francis Frith, Antonio Beato, and Felice Beato and James Robertson.

The photographs themselves are evidence of the rapid advances made in early photographic processes and testimony to the resilience and determination of traveling photographers. In spite of the extraordinary difficulties they encountered—heat, sand, and bulky equipment not the least among them—such was the number and dissemination of photographic images through prints, books, and stereoscopic views that in less than three decades, Egypt and the Middle East became an integral part of the European visual repertoire. In 1865, William Gifford Palgrave could refer to the colossi between Luxor and the Ramasseum as "well known to fame and photographists" (Frith, p. x).

CATALOGUE NO. 18.   Maxime Du Camp. *Nubie, Philoe, Temple Hipètre* from *Egypte, Nubie, Palestine et Syrie. Dessins photographiques recueillis pendant les années 1849, 1850 et 1851* (Paris: Gide et J. Baudry, 1852) pl. 70. Salted paper print; volume: 27.2 x 19 cm.

18

Maxime Du Camp, 1822–1894

Egypte, Nubie, Palestine et Syrie. Dessins photographiques recueillis pendant les années 1849, 1850 et 1851 accompagnés d'un texte explicatif

Paris: Gide et J. Baudry, 1852

125 salted paper prints from paper negatives, printed by the firm of Louis-Désiré Blanquart-Evrard of Lille; text printed by J. Claye et Cie of Paris; volume: 27.2 x 19 cm.

On display: "Nubie, Philoe, Temple Hipètre," plate 70

In November 1849, the young *littérateur* Maxime Du Camp, accompanied by his friend Gustave Flaubert, set off on an archaeological tour of Egypt, Nubia, and the Holy Land sponsored by the French Ministry of Education. Du Camp, who on previous trips had wasted valuable time sketching, needed an "instrument of precision to record [his] impressions if [he] was to reproduce them accurately" (Du Camp, 1893, vol. 1, p. 297). He took along photographic equipment, making use at first of Gustave Le Gray's dry waxed paper process. The results, possibly due to the heat, were disappointing. Following the advice of amateur photographer and travel acquaintance Baron Alexis de Lagrange, Du Camp switched to the wet paper process, which Louis-Désiré Blanquart-Evrard had recently adapted from Talbot's calotype process. The wet paper process was ideally suited for these climates and, during the following year, Du Camp photographed feverishly. He returned to France in 1851 with more than 200 negatives, which he entrusted for printing to the newly established firm of Blanquart-Evrard, in Lille.

One hundred and twenty-five of these photographs were selected for the book *Egypte, Nubie, Palestine et Syrie*, published in 1852. It was the first photographically illustrated book of this magnitude to be published in France. Issued in fascicles in an edition of 150 to 200 copies, and priced at 500 francs, the book met with respectable success. It stands to this day as a landmark of early photographic book illustration, admired for the quality and consistency of Blanquart-Evrard's production and, most important, for Du Camp's contribution. The combination of his unfettered eye and the soft tones of his medium grants his images a unique quality of drama and economy. *Egypte, Nubie, Palestine et Syrie* is Maxime Du Camp's sole contribution to photography.

19

Francis Frith, 1822–1898

Portion of the Great Hall of Columns at Karnak, ca. 1860

Stereoscopic albumen silver print on glass; 17.2 x 8.4 cm.
Signed and numbered in the negative: "Frith, 393"; descriptive printed label affixed to the glass at the left of the positive side

Francis Frith was born the same year as Maxime Du Camp to a middle-class family from Chesterfield, Derbyshire. By the time he came to photography at the age of 34, Frith had already established himself financially through a partnership in the grocery business and a thriving printing business in Liverpool. He embarked on a trip to Egypt in 1856, armed with a solid business plan and the latest photographic technique: he understood the increasing popular demand for topographical views of the grand tour and had mastered the relatively new wet collodion process.

CATALOGUE NO. 20.   Francis Frith. *View of the Memnonium at Thebes*, ca. 1860. Stereoscopic albumen silver print on glass; 17.2 x 8.4 cm.

The process, invented by Frederick Scott Archer in 1851, involved pouring collodion (a viscous solution of nitrocellulose in a mixture of ether and alcohol) onto a glass plate, which was sensitized with silver nitrate and exposed in the camera while still wet. The wet plate process was the most reliable and fastest photographic process at the time. It also gave remarkably sharp results as compared with the calotype. Nevertheless, the wet plate process remained very cumbersome, requiring that the plates be coated, sensitized, exposed, developed, and fixed in a very short period of time. It also required that the photographer carry equipment that was both fragile and extremely bulky.

It is all the more admirable that Frith, anticipating a range of publishing ventures, carried along three cameras, taking whole plate photographs (20.3 by 25.4 cm.), large-format views (40.6 by 50.8 cm.), and, as with this view of the Great Hall at Karnak, stereographs of the same sites.

20

Francis Frith, 1822–1898
View of the Memnonium at Thebes, ca. 1860
Stereoscopic albumen silver print on glass; 17.2 x 8.4 cm.
Signed and numbered in the negative: "Frith, 380"; descriptive printed label affixed to the glass

Possibly more than any other format, the stereoscopic view is evidence of the tremendous commercial expansion and domestication of photography between 1850 and 1860. The stereoscope—a binocular device in which two slightly offset angles of the same image are viewed in such a way that the two images merge together to form a single three-dimensional image—became widely popular after the Great Exhibition of 1851. It was at that exhibition that Jules Duboscq's fine instrument, used with daguerreotypes, was first displayed and noticed by throngs of spectators, including the Queen of England herself. The years that followed saw the rapid development and improvement of stereoscopic instruments and techniques and the distribution of thousands of views in millions of homes, both in Europe and in America. The Horblit collection, with its more than 670 views, is a rich resource for the study of stereoscopy.

Frith understood early on the possibilities of the new format. He returned in 1857 from his first trip to Egypt and the Holy Land with more than a hundred stereoscopic negatives, capturing additional views on each subsequent voyage. He entrusted them to the leading London stereographic firm of Negretti and Zambra, which issued them as both glass and card stereoscopic views. In 1860, Frith established his own firm, F. Frith and Company, in Reigate, Surrey, to produce and distribute his work. The Horblit collection contains nine of Frith's prints and eight of his stereoscopic views. His firm continued to offer Egyptian and Palestinian views long after Frith's death in 1898, and went on to publish postcards until the 1960s.

21

Antonio Beato, died 1903

Temple of Karnak, 1860s.

Albumen silver print; image: 28 x 21.4 cm., mount: 45.7 x 35.5 cm.

Signed on the negative: A. Beato

The Beato brothers, Felice and Antonio, occupy a special place in the history of photography in Egypt and the Middle East. In a period of increasing commercialism, they found a niche by establishing studios and selling and distributing from abroad rather than from Europe. Of the two, Felice is the better known, in particular for his association with James Robertson, his brother-in-law, and their photographic coverage of the Crimean War (1855) and views of Athens, Malta, Constantinople, and Egypt.

Antonio Beato cut a lesser figure. He opened a studio in Cairo in 1860–61, moving the following year to Luxor, where he worked till his death in the early 1900s. In Luxor, Antonio made a living by photographing archaeological expeditions and catering to tourists. Though his shop remained small, an inventory of his belongings reveals that he owned six lenses, three cameras, more than 1,500 negatives, and several thousand postcards at the time of his death. Prolific by necessity, he photographed the same sites several times during his career, continually updating his stock in what was already a very competitive market.

Antonio's early views, in particular those of Cairo, are noted for their amateurish quality. His mature style, as exemplified by this view of Karnak, takes advantage of what have become standard tricks of the trade—the dramatic angle delineating monumental masses, while a play of light and shadow strongly articulates them, and the use of native figures and their mounts strategically placed within the ruins. Yet, the whole retains, as does most of Antonio's work, an unaffected quality and a truly natural charm.

CATALOGUE NO. 21.   Antonio Beato. *Temple of Karnak*, 1860s. Albumen silver print; image: 28 x 21.4 cm., mount: 45.7 x 35.5 cm.

22

Richard Morris Hunt, 1828–1895

Temple of Karnak, 1853

Salted paper print from a paper negative; image: 23.7 x 19.4 cm., mount: 48.9 x 37 cm.

The American Richard Morris Hunt moved to Europe in 1843, at the age of sixteen, in the company of his widowed mother and four siblings. The next ten years were a rich period of learning and travel for the young man. He settled on architecture as his field of interest and apprenticed at the *ateliers* of Thomas Couture and Hector-Martin Lefuel. Hunt was the first American to train at l'École des Beaux-Arts in Paris. In 1852, he set off on an architectural grand tour that took him from the Loire Valley to southern Europe, Egypt, and the Near East. All along the way he sketched monuments and kept detailed notes. He also took photographs, a skill he might have learned from his younger brother Leavitt, who had just returned from his own tour the preceding year.

Hunt arrived in Egypt in 1853. A note in his Nile diary mentions that "the bugs, vermin, etc. are insupportable, gentlemen are terribly discomforted. This is the country to read about, not visit" (Howard, p. 29). His photographs nevertheless demonstrate a keen interest in the people and in the monuments.

Hunt's views—six of which are in the Horblit collection—were intended not for a commercial audience but simply for his own pleasure and study. They are surprisingly sophisticated. The bold angle, for example, at which he captures the temple of Karnak anticipates by close to a decade Antonio Beato's formula. The absence of human figures and the soft tones of the salted paper process give this particular view a dreamy, almost otherworldly quality.

CATALOGUE NO. 26a.   Philip Henry Delamotte. *Crystal Palace at Sydenham, Interior View*, ca. 1854.
Albumen silver print; image: 21.3 x 16.8 cm., mount: 34 x 27.9 cm.

CASE 5

The Great Exhibition of 1851

The year 1851 was a turning point in the history of photography. It was the year of Daguerre's death, the year Archer announced his collodion process, and the year the first photographic society, the Société Héliographique, was formed. Talbot was experimenting with the first instantaneous photographs using electric spark illumination, Gustave Le Gray had announced his waxed-paper process, and Niepce de Saint-Victor was perfecting the use of albumen for positive prints. It was also the year of the world's first international exhibition, where photography from Europe and the United States was introduced to an international audience.

The idea of "a self-supporting exhibition of the products of British industry" was discussed for many years but it was Prince Albert who finally developed the concept into an international exposition. The Great Exhibition, as it came to be known, was sponsored by the Society for the Encouragement of Arts, Manufactures, and Commerce (called the Society of Arts), of which the Prince Consort was president. The exhibition was housed in the Crystal Palace, a glass and iron structure designed by Sir Joseph Paxton and constructed in London's Hyde Park. On May 1, 1851, the exhibition was inaugurated by Queen Victoria herself. More than six million people visited over the next five months.

The exhibition was divided into four main sections: raw materials, machinery and mechanical inventions, manufactures, and sculpture and the plastic arts. In the Crystal Palace, photographs could be found throughout the building, while in the subsequent catalogue, *Reports of the Juries*, they are chiefly discussed under class X: philosophical instruments and processes depending upon their use, and, to a lesser extent, in class XXX: fine arts. Daguerreotypes and paper prints were both exhibited. At this time, the negative was considered the work of art; in the show's catalogue, for example, the positive prints are referred to as proofs. Of the ten prize medals given for photography, the French, praised for their paper photography, won four; the Americans won three and were acclaimed for their daguerreotypes; the British won two; and the Austrians received one.

23

Portraits of British Royalty, Statesmen, and Celebrities

Unpublished album, ca. 1863

46 *cartes de visite;* volume: 20 x 16 cm.

From the collection of Sir Thomas Phillipps

On display: Portrait of Prince Albert and *Portrait of Queen Victoria*, both by John Jabez Edwin Mayall

Of all the planners, organizers, and sponsors of the Great Exhibition, Prince Albert was the most influential. In 1851, Albert was 32 years old and had been married to Victoria for 11 years, but it was only after the exhibition opened that he became known and loved by the British public. *The Art-Journal* dedicated its *Illustrated Catalogue* of the exhibition to Albert: "It is difficult to assign to Prince Albert the degree of praise which is really his due on this occasion without incurring the suspicion of being in some degree influenced by the exalted position he holds in the country" (pp. xiii–xiv).

Albert and Victoria visited the Crystal Palace often, devoting much of their attention to the photographic exhibits. They became avid collectors of photographs and had the negatives they owned printed by the dozens as gifts. A portable darkroom and printing room were brought to Windsor Castle, to accommodate the many photographers who were invited to photograph the royal family. More than anything else, it was this enthusiasm shown by the royal family that spurred the rapid progress and popularity of photography during the 1850s. In the year following the Great Exhibition, the Photographic Society was formed in London, the first issue of the *Photographic Journal* was published, and the first international exhibition devoted entirely to photography was held at the Society of Arts.

This small *carte de visite* album in red morocco leather is one of six originally owned by Sir Thomas Phillipps and purchased by Horblit from the Robinson Brothers around 1961. The Phillipps albums contain *cartes de visite* by a variety of photographers, including John Jabez Edwin Mayall, Disdéri & Cie, William Edward Kilburn, Maull & Polyblank, Camille Silvy, and L. Haase & Co. of Berlin. The portraits depict such notables as Florence Nightingale, Lord Palmerston, Lord Macaulay, and Lord Stanley, as well as members of the British royal family.

24a

The Great Exhibition of the Works of Industry of All Nations, 1851. Reports by the Juries on the Subjects in the Thirty Classes into which the Exhibition was Divided

London: Spicer Brothers, wholesale stationers; W. Clowes and Sons, printers; contractors to the Royal Commission, 1852. 4 vols.

154 salted paper prints; volume: 36 x 27.8 cm.

One of an edition of 140; previously owned by Lord Overstone

On display: "Class X. Philosophical Instruments and Processes Depending upon Their Use," opposite a photograph captioned, *Electro-Magnetic Apparatus and Theodolite* [invented by] *Froment*, pp. 518–19

24b

The Great Exhibition of the Works of Industry of All Nations, 1851. Official Descriptive and Illustrated Catalogue

London: Spicer Brothers, wholesale stationers; W. Clowes and Sons, printers; contractors to the Royal Commission, 1852. 3 vols.

Illustrations include steel engravings after daguerreotypes; volume: 36 x 27.8 cm.

One of an edition of 140; previously owned by Lord Overstone

On display: cover

CLASS X.

PHILOSOPHICAL INSTRUMENTS AND PROCESSES DEPENDING UPON THEIR USE.

Jury.

Sir DAVID BREWSTER, F.R.S., *Chairman*, St. Andrews, Fifeshire, N.B.: Principal of the University, St. Andrews.

Professor COLLADON, Switzerland.

E. B. DENISON, 42 Queen Anne Street.

J. GLAISHER, F.R.S., *Reporter*, 13 Dartmouth Terrace, Lewisham; Observer in Greenwich Observatory.

Sir JOHN HERSCHEL, Bart., F.R.S., 32 Harley Street; Master of the Mint.

Professor HETSCH, Denmark.

E. R. LESLIE, R.A., United States; Artist.

L. MATHIEU, France; Member of Bureau of Longitude, of Institute, and of Central Jury.

W. H. MILLER, F.R.S., Scroope Terrace, Cambridge; Professor of Mineralogy.

RICHARD POTTER., A.M., University College, London; Professor of Natural Philosophy.

Professor SCHUBARTH, Zollverein; Professor of Chemistry and Natural Philosophy.

Baron ARMAND SEGUIER, France; Member of Institute, &c.

Associates.

J. S. BOWERBANK, 3 Highbury Grove.

Rev. W. S. KINGSLEY, Sidney College, Cambridge; Fellow of Sidney College.

L. A. J. QUETELET, Belgium; Secretary to the Royal Academy at Brussels. (Juror in Class XXX.)

Lord WROTTESLEY, 34 St. James's Place.

THE duties of the Jury upon Philosophical Instruments have been found to be very heavy, as indeed might be expected in a field so vast, including instruments relating to Astronomy, Optics, Light, Heat, Electricity, Magnetism, Acoustics, Meteorology, &c.; in fact, all relating to Physical Science, collected by a large number of exhibitors.

Astronomical instruments claim our first attention; the exhibitors of which, though few in number, have effected a most beneficial advance by the use of as few parts in their construction as possible: this is mainly observable in the British portion. The workmanship of those exhibited by Germany deserves the highest praise: the instruments are, however, few in number, and do not fully represent German art.

America claims particular notice by the application of electro-magnetism to the registration of astronomical observations, thus enabling the hand to do the work of the mind. This method has the further advantage of being able to record the observations taken at far-separated Observatories, the length of the wire used being immaterial: thus is established a means the best possible for the determination of the difference of longitude. Observatories so connected afford the means of

3 Z

CATALOGUE NO. 24a   "Class X, Philosophical Instruments and Processes Depending upon Their Use," from *The Great Exhibition of the Works of Industry of All Nations, 1851. Reports by the Juries* (London: Spicer Brothers, 1852) vol. 2, pp. 518–19. Volume: 36 x 27.8 cm.

Before the Great Exhibition closed, a royal commission was formed to prepare a catalogue. In keeping with the grand scale of the event, a lavish set of eight volumes was presented to members of the Royal Court, the Royal Commission, and a few foreign dignitaries. Each set included the *Descriptive and Illustrated Catalogue*, in three volumes, the *Jury Reports*, in four volumes, and one volume of various *Reports to the Crown*. Steel engravings were used to illustrate the *Descriptive Catalogue*, many of them after daguerreotypes by J. J. E. Mayall, Richard Beard, Antoine Claudet, and others.

Under the leadership of Charles Thurston Thompson, the decision was made to use photographs as illustrations for the *Jury Reports*. The initial plan was to give the commission to Nicolaas Henneman, previously Talbot's assistant, now managing his own firm in London with Thomas Malone. Hugh Owen of Bristol had already made a number of negatives, and through Henneman, arrangements were made to have Friedrich von Martens, Claude Marie Ferrier, and Robert Bingham assist him in photographing the Great Exhibition, its building, and surrounding gardens.

Throughout the fall of 1851, Talbot negotiated on behalf of Henneman for the contract to print the catalogue illustrations. Although Talbot, who still maintained the calotype copyright, offered to make concessions for Henneman, Talbot failed to win the printing commission for his friend. The job of printing the 21,700 photographs for the 140 copies of the *Jury Reports* went to Robert Bingham, who took the assignment to the south of France. There in the bright and predictable sun, mass printing could be done at a much lower cost than in England. Bingham later settled in Paris and built a thriving commercial photography business. Talbot was compensated with 15 copies of the catalogue.

25a
British School

Great Exhibition Hyde Park, ca. 1854
Stereoscopic albumen silver print on glass; 8.5 x 17.3 cm.
Written on glass plate, "DL" or "DJ"; title from printed paper label.

25b

Henry Negretti, 1818–1879, and Joseph Warren Zambra, born 1822
Stereoscopic View of John Bell's "Una and the Lion" at the Crystal Palace
London: Negretti & Zambra, ca. 1854
Stereoscopic daguerreotype; 8.3 x 17.3 cm.
Label on verso reads, "Photographers to the Crystal Palace Company, H. Negretti & Zambra, Meteorological Instrument Makers, and Opticians, no. 11, Hatton Garden, London"

25c

British School

Stereoscopic View of the Elizabethan Court at the Crystal Palace

London, ca. 1854

Stereoscopic daguerreotype; 8.3 x 17.3 cm.

Label on verso reads, "No. 8. The Elizabethan Court [added in pen by Horblit: at the Crystal Palace, London]. Holland House, Kensington, supplied the models for the facades and arcades of this Court; the two bronze figures in the Nave, by Taddeo Landini, are from the fountain of the Tartarughi, or of the Tortoises at Rome; the bust in the distance is that of Shakespeare from his monument at Stratford; that nearer to the left is Francis I; the tomb is from Wimborne in Dorsetshire, without a name"

The partnership of Henry Negretti and Joseph Zambra was formed around 1850. One of their first jobs was to create optical and meteorological instruments for the Royal Observatory at the request of Prince Albert. The instruments were exhibited at the Great Exhibition, for which they received a prize medal. Negretti and Zambra became one of the most successful technical instrument businesses in London, selling cameras and optical devices, darkroom equipment, and chemicals, as well as photographic prints, magic lantern slides, and stereoscopic views on glass and paper. Negretti and Zambra were given the franchise for photographing the Crystal Palace (which had been recreated in Sydenham) and had an optical shop inside the building. Although both Negretti and Zambra knew how to make photographs, they found commercial success publishing

CATALOGUE NO. 25a.   British School. *Great Exhibition Hyde Park*, ca. 1854. Stereoscopic albumen silver prints on glass; 8.3 x 17.3 cm.

the work of other artists, such as Francis Frith, Philip Delamotte, and in particular, Claude-Marie Ferrier's glass stereoscopic views of the Crystal Palace. Negretti went on to make the first aerial photographs in England, staging a well-publicized balloon ride over Sydenham in 1863.

26a

Philip Henry Delamotte, 1820–1889

Crystal Palace at Sydenham, Interior View, ca. 1854

Albumen silver print; image: 21.3 x 16.8 cm., mount: 34 x 27.7 cm.

26b

Philip Henry Delamotte, 1820–1889

Crystal Palace at Sydenham, View of North Transept, ca. 1854

Albumen silver print; image: 20 x 16.8 cm., mount: 34.8 x 27.9 cm.

The Great Exhibition of 1851 was so popular that after it closed, the building was dismantled and the parts transported to Sydenham, 12 miles south of London, where it was reconstructed beginning in 1852. The relocated building, which was opened to the public in June 1854, was meant to house a permanent version of the Great Exhibition. Philip H. Delamotte, son of the painter William De La Motte, is the photographer connected most closely with this building. Delamotte was a commercial illustrator and drawing instructor who learned to make photographs in the late 1840s. He quickly became one of London's leading practitioners and teachers, and in 1852, along with Roger Fenton, received critical praise for his work at the first exhibition devoted to photography. Delamotte began to advertise himself as a photographic documenter, which made him the obvious choice to capture photographically the rebuilding of the Crystal Palace in Sydenham. Delamotte was subsequently named the official photographer of the Crystal Palace Company, and his work used in numerous publications, including *Views of the Crystal Palace and Park, Guide to the Crystal Palace and Park*, and his own *Photographic Reports of the Progress of the Crystal Palace at Sydenham*, published with Joseph Cundall. The Horblit collection contains only four Delamotte photographs: three of the Crystal Palace and one taken in Wales.

Delamotte wrote one of the early photography handbooks, *The Practice of Photography*, which was published in 1853 by his partner Joseph Cundall, an art historian, photographer, and publisher of children's books. There are two copies of this important early manual in the Horblit collection: one owned by Sir Thomas Phillipps and one by G. W. Ashworth, who bought his directly from the author and made copious notes on Delamotte's formulas in the margins. Cundall and Delamotte advertised five other volumes in 1853: *Photographic Studies* by George Shaw; Delamotte's *Crystal Palace; A Series of Photographic Pictures* by Hugh Owen; *A Series of Photographic Pictures of Welsh Scenery* by J. D. Llewellyn; and *The Photographic Album*, with photographs by Fenton, Delamotte, Alfred Rosling, Owen, and Cundall. The Horblit collection also contains Cundall's own *Twenty Views in Gloucestershire* (1854).

CATALOGUE NO. 26b.   Philip Henry Delamotte. *Crystal Palace at Sydenham, View of North Transept,* ca. 1854. Albumen silver print; image: 20 x 16.8 cm.

CATALOGUE NO. 28.   H. G. DeBurlo. *The Graff House*, 1855. Albumen silver print from a negative by
Frederic DeBourg Richards; image: 20.5 x 15.3 cm., mount: 38 x 29.3 cm.

CASE 6

Americans and Paper Photography

Photographers from the United States are represented in the Horblit collection not only by daguerreotypes but also by a rich group of salted paper and albumen silver prints, primarily from Boston and Philadelphia. Along with New York City and Washington D.C., these cities were the American centers of early commercial photography, where photographic studios opened in the early 1840s on the most fashionable streets. Photographers such as the Langenheim brothers in Philadelphia began making paper negatives and prints as early as 1842, and although their greatest commercial success was with daguerreotypes, they also chose to exhibit their Talbotypes in the Great Exhibition of 1851. Many amateur photographers experimented with paper throughout the heyday of daguerreotypes, and with the transition from copper to glass plate, the American public began to demand photographs on paper. The Horblit collection contains examples of paper prints by many of the most notable American photographers, such as Southworth and Hawes, Whipple and Black, Frederick DeBourg Richards, John B. Greene, Richard Morris Hunt, and James McClees. Photographs of San Francisco's Chinatown, Tiffany's windows on Fifth Avenue in New York City, and Pepper's Brewery in Philadelphia, along with many others, provide a vibrant record of American cities in the middle of the nineteenth century.

27
Frederick Langenheim, 1809–1879, and
William Langenheim, 1807–1874 (attributed to)

John W. Cooper, Pharmacist at McAllister Brothers, Philadelphia, 1859

Stereoscopic albumenized salted paper print; image: 7.6 x 14.4 cm., mount: 8.6 x 16.5 cm.

The Langenheim brothers were Philadelphia entrepreneurs. They began their photography business selling the cameras and photographic equipment of Peter Voigtländer (who later became their brother-in-law). The brothers taught themselves to make daguerreotypes, opening a commercial studio in 1842 (see below R43). In 1846, they found a way to project their photographs and invited the public into their studio to view them for a small admission charge. The Langenheim brothers purchased the rights to Talbot's calotype process in 1849 and attempted to market licenses in the United States (leading to bankruptcy in 1851). They subsequently perfected stereoscopic photography and by 1854 were mass-producing stereographs on glass and paper. The following year, the brothers welcomed the public into their new studio on Chestnut Street to see, for twenty-five cents, their stereoscopic views projected by a Cosmorama.

At the other end of Chestnut Street was their competitor, McAllister brothers' optical supply store. A large number of Langenheim photographs survive of the McAllisters and their shop, suggesting the families were on good terms. This stereoscopic view of John W. Cooper sitting at a table shows many of the instruments available at the McAllisters' shop—a compound microscope, an electrostatic device, a spyglass, spectacles, a gyroscope, a globe, and a tide dial, which

CATALOGUE NO. 27. Frederick and William Langenheim (attributed to). *John W. Cooper, Pharmacist at McAllister Brothers, Philadelphia,* 1859. Stereoscopic albumenized salted paper print; image: 7.6 x 14.4 cm., mount: 8.6 x 16.5 cm.

showed the daily change in the tides when the crank was turned. A second view, owned by the Library Company of Philadelphia, shows John McAllister, Jr. (father of the brothers who ran the shop) sitting at the same table of instruments.

28

Frederic DeBourg Richards, 1822–1903

The Graff House, 1855

Salted paper print; image: 20.5 x 15.3 cm., mount: 38 x 29.3 cm.

Thomas Jefferson rented the second floor of Jacob Graff's house at Market and Seventh Streets in Philadelphia during the summer of 1776, and wrote the Declaration of Independence at this location. This fact, established in the 1850s by amateur historian John McAllister, Jr., led to the building's designation as the "Birth Place of Liberty." McAllister was a friend and patron to many young photographers, who often came to the family optical shop for photographic lenses and other equipment. McAllister urged them to photograph Philadelphia's historic sites and may have encouraged Richards to capture the Graff House before it was changed by its newfound celebrity.

The Horblit collection includes one daguerreotype and twenty-six paper prints by Richards, who began his career as a landscape painter. He continued to have success exhibiting his paintings while at the same time establishing himself as one of Philadelphia's leading daguerreotypists. Richards was also an early master of paper photography and formed a partnership with John Betts to sell all contemporary formats, including ambrotypes. In addition to this print, the Horblit collection contains a second, albumen print of the Graff House, by H. G. DeBurlo, made from the same negative (shown in this catalogue). The Library Company of Philadelphia owns a similar photograph of the house taken later the same year by James McClees. In the McClees photograph, a brightly striped awning has been added to the building, announcing the connection with Jefferson, and a sign on the third floor advertising cheap office space has been removed.

29

John Adams Whipple, 1822–1891 (attributed to)

Homes of American Statesmen: with Anecdotical, Personal, and Descriptive Sketches by Various Writers, Illustrated with Engravings on Wood from Drawings by Döpler and Daguerreotypes, and Fac-similes of Autograph Letters

New York, G.P. Putnam and Company, 1854
Illustrations include one salted paper print; volume: 21 x 15 cm.

On display: Hancock House, Boston, an original sun picture, frontispiece: title from pencil inscription

The Horblit collection has two copies of this book, and the view of the Hancock House is slightly different in each. One book is inscribed, "Thos. C. Doremus, Esq./with the most affec. & grateful love & Christmas greetings for his sister/Henretta B. Haines/Dec. 25, 1853," indicating that the book was available before the 1854 publication date. Similar inscriptions in other copies have led historians to maintain that this was the first photographically illustrated book published in America, preceding *Remarks on Some Fossil Impressions* (a copy of this volume, published in 1854, is also part of the Horblit collection). The publishers highlight this photograph in their preface, "The frontispiece is somewhat of a curiosity, *each copy* being an *original sun-picture* on paper. The great luminary has here entered into direct competition with other artists in the engraving business."

John Adams Whipple began making daguerreotypes in the winter of 1839–40. His patents for "crayon portraiture" (1849) and "crystalotypes" (1850) established him as a leading talent in nineteenth-century photography. Historians attribute this photograph to Whipple on the basis of his blind stamp indicating a crystalotype negative, which appears on prints in some copies of *Homes*, although not in Horblit's books. The Horblit collection contains a similar photograph of the Hancock House made by James Wallace Black, Whipple's partner at the time, who specialized in architectural photography. It is reasonable to assume that Black was the actual photographer and that his work was published under the studio's name using Whipple's blind stamp.

30

James Wallace Black, 1825–1896 (attributed to)

Old John Hancock House, Boston, between 1858 and 1863

Albumen silver print; image: 41 x 30 cm., mount: 45.2 x 35 cm.

The Hancock House was Boston's first stone house, built by Thomas Hancock in 1737, the year his nephew John Hancock was born. It stood until 1863 at 30 Beacon Street on what is today the eastern extension of the State House grounds. The streetlights seen in this photograph have a flat bottom and clear glass, indicating that they are not the earliest model and helping to establish the date of the view some time after 1857. A similar, but earlier view credited to John Whipple was used as the frontispiece for *Homes of American Statesmen* (see above no. 29). During the 1850s, the rapid growth and transformation of Boston's neighborhoods was a common subject for the city's photographers. James Black established a reputation for his architectural studies and often photographed prominent Boston buildings shortly before their demolition.

Black was a partner in Whipple's Boston studio from 1850 to 1859 and perfected Whipple's crystalotype process, teaching the technique to many others, including Oliver Wendell Holmes and Josiah Johnson Hawes. Black is credited with taking the first aerial photographs in the United States and helped to establish the Boston Photographic Union in 1869. The enormous respect Black's peers had for his work can be seen in the comments of Marcus Root, who wrote, "Mr. Black's success for the last five years in all branches of his profession, is probably without a parallel in the United States at this date (1863). He has one of the most extensive and best-planned establishments, now existing, for every department of the art" (Root, p. 381).

CATALOGUE NO. 31.   William James Stillman. *The Old Churchyard* from *Poetic Localities of Cambridge* (Boston: James R. Osgood and Company, 1876), pl. 35. Heliotype from a negative by Stillman; volume: 25 x 19.5 cm.

31
William James Stillman, 1828–1901

Poetic Localities of Cambridge

Edited by W. J. Stillman; text by Oliver Wendell Holmes, Henry Wadsworth Longfellow, and James Russell Lowell; heliotypes printed from negatives by William James Stillman
Boston: James R. Osgood and Company, 1876
12 heliotypes; volume: 25 x 19.5 cm.

On display: The Old Churchyard, plate 36

William James Stillman was a Pre-Raphaelite painter, journalist, and editor of the first American art journal, *The Crayon*. He bought his first camera in 1857, "a rude, inefficient, and cumbersome apparatus and process for field-work, of which few amateurs nowadays can conceive the inconveniences" (Stillman, vol. 1, p. 239). He received two lessons from James Black, of the Boston firm of Whipple and Black. Throughout his career as a journalist, Stillman continued to practice photography and, while working in London as a foreign correspondent, wrote *The Amateur's Photographic Guide Book* (1874).

While the printer, or heliotyper, of the photographs in *Poetic Localities of Cambridge* is unknown, the negatives were all made by Stillman. They were taken during a trip to New England in the summer of 1874 with his son, who was terminally ill. Stillman writes in his preface, "In the hope that I may preserve them for another generation, I have photographed some of those [places] which belong to Cambridge. This I have taken on myself to do, though no child of hers, but only a vagabond guest made free of her fields and memories, and not unknown in some of the houses which are her pride, that I may thereby pay my tribute of reverent admiration where the muse has given her highest favors." For this exhibition, the book is open to a view of Christ Church, built in 1760 on Garden Street, photographed from the Old Burying Ground.

32
American School

Brattle Square Church, Showing Slave Gallery Behind the Organ, 1850s
Salted paper print; image: 19.2 x 24.5 cm., mount: 29 x 34.4 cm.

The first Brattle Square Church was built in 1699 on a piece of land in Boston called the Brattle Close. Although Thomas Brattle left money in his will to provide the church with "a pair of organs," its members voted against having music during their worship. In 1772, John Hancock proposed a complete renovation of the church, and a new building was constructed on the same site. The question of music during public worship was again raised and this time the vote passed but on condition that the organ be purchased by voluntary subscription. (One parishioner secretly offered to pay the entire cost, if the organ could be accidentally dropped into the Boston harbor during its unloading, but his offer was not accepted.)

The title of the photograph refers to the upper gallery "appropriated to colored persons" (Lothrop, p. 148), which is seen at the top of the photograph, behind the organ pipes. This seating area once projected out as far as the middle gallery but was shortened to make room for the organ, thereby cutting the number of seats for black parishioners in half. The addition of the clock was the church's last renovation, in 1811. As the neighborhood deteriorated, a decision was made to move the congregation to a new site, and in 1869 this building was destroyed. The new Brattle Square Church, designed by H. H. Richardson, was constructed on Commonwealth Avenue at Clarendon Street, and opened in 1873.

CASE 7

Souvenirs from Italy

Ever since the Renaissance, Italy has been a favorite destination for travelers; a trip to Italy was even considered, in some milieus, an essential part of a gentleman's education. Collecting mementos was an important part of the trip, and while some visitors did their own sketches or paintings, most purchased topographical views and reproductions of works of arts. The demand for mementos created a lucrative market for painters and especially printmakers, who, over the centuries, established large production centers and distribution networks throughout Italy and beyond.

The demand for mementos explains the extraordinarily rapid dissemination of photography in Italy in the second part of the nineteenth century. Two decades at most separate the work of amateur calotypists sojourning in Rome in the early 1850s from the thousands of albumen prints produced by commercial photographers—both Italian and foreign-born—to satisfy the ever-growing tourist market in the 1860s and 1870s.

The Horblit collection is particularly rich in early Italian photographs: from Rome, the prints of Robert Macpherson and Count Frédéric Flachéron; from Florence, the photographs of the Fratelli Alinari; from Venice, those of Carlo Naya and Carlo Ponti; and from Naples, the work of Giorgio Sommer and Giacomo Arena, to name a few. The numerous city views, genre scenes, reproductions of works of art and Greco-Roman antiquities illustrate, better than any other medium could, the Italian scene of the time. But just as important, these prints and paper and glass-plate negatives document the rapid technical developments in Italian photography, its progressive dominance over traditional printmaking, and the development of a new aesthetic, a fresh way of looking and remembering.

CATALOGUE NO. 33.   Frédéric A. Flachéron. *Cloître de St. Jean de Latran*, Rome, 1890s? Albumen silver print from a paper negative by Frédéric A. Flachéron; image: 15 x 18.7 cm., mount: 27.7 x 38.7 cm.

33
Frédéric A. Flachéron, 1813–1883

Cloître de St. Jean de Latran, **Rome, 1890s?**

Albumen silver print from a paper negative by Frédéric A. Flachéron; 15 x 18.7 cm., mount: 27.7 x 38.7 cm.
Title inscribed in ink in a contemporary hand on lower left of mount; stamped in lower right: "Vente Flacheron, 4 Juin 1987, Vendome"

The Caffè Greco, located near the Spanish steps, was by all accounts the favorite meeting place of artists, architects, and archaeologists residing or sojourning in Rome in the mid-nineteenth century. It was there that a small circle of amateur photographers—the first such group recorded in Italy—met regularly in the early 1850s. The Roman Circle, as it came to be known, counted among its most prominent members the sculptor and painter Count Frédéric A. Flachéron, the painter Eugène Constant, and Prince Giron des Anglonnes. Also associated with the group were the architect Alfred-Nicolas Normand, then laureate of the Académie de France in residence at the Villa Medicis, and Giacomo Caneva, who trained as a painter in Padua and moved to Rome in the late 1830s. An extended essay entitled "Roman Views," by Andrew Szegedy-Maszak, appears in the companion volume to this catalogue, *Six Exposures: Essays in Celebration of the Opening of the Harrison D. Horblit Collection of Early Photography.*

The members of the Roman Circle shared a fascination with the Eternal City and an active interest in the new medium of photography. While some had previously made daguerreotypes, all were experimenting now with the wet calotype process, adapted by Blanquart-Evrard from the original dry process developed by Talbot. Richard W. Thomas, a photographic wholesaler from London, gave an interesting account of his visit to Rome and his encounter with the group in 1852 (*The Art-Journal*, new ser., vol. 4 [1852], p. 159). Thomas, who arrived fully equipped with the tools necessary for the Talbot process, failed to match the excellent results he had obtained in England, a failure he correctly blamed on the hot climate and strong light of the peninsula. While on an excursion to Tivoli, he met Giron des Anglonnes and Caneva, who taught him the wet process as it was practiced by the Roman Circle and introduced him to their calotypist friends at the Caffè Greco.

Among the practitioners at the Caffè Greco, Flachéron acquired early on an international reputation—some of his views were greatly admired in London, at the Great Exhibition of 1851 and at the Society of Arts exhibition of 1852. The ample composition, scale, and warm honey hues of this photograph are representative of both the aesthetic and the technique of the Roman Circle at the time. In addition to this view, his print of the *North West Corner of the Roman Forum*, 1850, is also on display (see below H1). There are more than 80 Flachéron prints in the Horblit collection and 37 of his paper negatives. Conservator Lee Ann Daffner recently completed an analysis of the paper negatives, which throws new light on Flachéron's technique and his contribution to the art of the calotype.

CATALOGUE NO. 34.   Carlo Ponti. *Palais la Ca' d'Oro* from *Souvenir photographique de Venise* (Venice: Chez Charles Ponti, ca. 1860). Albumen silver prints; volume: 36 x 46.5 cm.

34
Carlo Ponti, ca. 1823–1893

Souvenir photographique de Venise

Venise: Chez Charles Ponti, opticien, Riva degli Schiavoni, no. 4180 [ca. 1860]
Binding title: *Ricordo di Venezia*
Album containing a lithographed title page and 15 albumen silver prints with decorative mounts, each titled on the back, in French, in a contemporary hand; volume: 36 x 46.5 cm.

On display: Pont Rialto and *Palais la Ca' d'Oro*

Carlo Ponti, a native of Sagno in the Swiss Tessino, settled in Venice as a young man. There he worked as an optical instrument maker and a photographer till the end of his days. Renowned for his fine lenses, he was celebrated in particular for his invention of the Megalethoscope—a panoramic photograph viewer with rear illumination—and its larger version, the Alethoscope, which earned him the Grand Prize at the Universal Exhibition of London in 1862. When Venice became part of Italy, in 1866, Ponti lost his patent for the Alethoscope. His collaborator, Carlo Naya, began producing the instrument under his own name, prompting Ponti to sever his ties with Naya and to sue him for infringement of rights.

Today, Ponti is best remembered for his views of Venice where he was the first photographer to establish a commercial enterprise. In 1855, he presented a series of 160 photographic views at the Universal Exhibition in Paris and received a medal in recognition of his work. His ample and carefully composed *vedute* capture in all their details the intricate lace of the palazzo facades, the rough texture of the stone bridges, and the damp shadows of the passageways. The absence of passersby—too swift for the camera to capture—and the motionless glow of the canal give Ponti's scenes a serene and timeless quality. There are 38 of his photographs in the Horblit collection.

In the 1860s, Ponti began to sell albums of photographs such as this one. A traveler might have selected some twenty views from Ponti's stock, including Ponti's own but also some from Carlo Naya, whose photographs Ponti published and edited from the mid-1850s to the mid-1860s, and from other Venetian photographers such as Antonio Fortunato Perini and Giuseppe Coen. Although the binding of this album, stamped in gold, bears the standard Italian title, *Ricordo di Venezia*, the lithographic title page indicates that the album was intended for a French-speaking customer. The owner has carefully labeled the back of each photograph in French.

35
Giorgio Sommer, 1834–1914

Marina de Messina, Sicily, ca. 1867

Albumen silver print; 19 x 25.5 cm.

In 1857, the young Giorgio Sommer, native of Frankfurt am Main, established himself in Naples after working for a brief period as a professional photographer in Switzerland. Several commercial photographers were already active in Naples at the time, among them Roberto Rive and the Frenchmen Alphonse Bernoud and J. Grillet. From the start, Sommer showed himself to be an ambitious and gifted entrepreneur. In 1860, he established a partnership with Edmondo Behles, another German-born photographer, who had an active practice in Rome. Over the next twelve years they developed a large repertoire of views and built an international distribution network rivaling that of the large photographic studios in the north.

During the 1860s and 1870s, Sommer systematically photographed the major cities of the Italian peninsula, venturing even to Malta. He assembled one of the most extensive collections of views and reproductions of artwork of the time. His *Catalogo di fotografie d'Italia e Malta* was published in 1873, just in time for the Universal Exhibition in Vienna. The catalogue included portraits, genre scenes, and a number of striking photographs of Pompeii. In 1874, the American traveler Edward L. Wilson noted, "In Naples, the largest producer [of photography] is Mr. Sommer. Mr. Sommer has a very extensive salesroom on one of the principal streets, where a very fine display is made. [His establishment] is supplied with all the necessities for making excellent results in any quantity" (Coke, p. 22).

Listed as no. 1353 in Sommer's *Catalogo di fotografie* is this photograph of the Marina de Messina. Like most of Sommer's photographs, 16 of which are in the Horblit collection, this view is remarkable for the economy of its composition. The sweeping semicircle of the marina fronted by handsome buildings is beautifully balanced by the Neptune fountain with its octagonal basin and heavy railing. It might be early morning—the coffee houses are still closed. The small boats are tethered, the fluttering of their lowered sails echoing that of the shops' awnings. Barrels and chariot lie idle, while a few men gathered in shadowy groups confer. Sommer's photograph grants the beholder a privileged view of the city before it awakens. Best of all, in the words of Mr. Wilson, the visitor may, with a simple purchase, "carry away the shadow of the things which he has seen in these curious places" (ibid).

CATALOGUE NO. 35.   Giorgio Sommer. *Marina de Messina, Sicily*, ca. 1867. Albumen silver print; 19 x 25.5 cm.

36
Giacomo Arena, 1821–1906

Giacomo Arena and Staff Photographing Outdoors in an Unidentified Landscape, ca. 1861

Albumen silver print; image: 14 x 21.8 cm., mount: 26.3 x 36.3 cm.
Stamped on the back of the mount: "ARENA 7 Strada Pace Napoli"

The Horblit collection's extensive holdings of the prints, negatives, and photographic apparatus of Giacomo Arena, active in his native city of Naples from the 1860s to the 1880s, allow us to examine the work of a studio quite different from that of his Neapolitan colleague and contemporary, Giorgio Sommer. Arena's practice was smaller, and though some of his views were intended for the tourist trade, the bulk of his work was done for the local market. As a result, his photographs have a distinct provincial flavor.

Arena's work in the Horblit collection includes the obligatory prints of city monuments, topographical views, and archaeological sites of Pompeii intended for tourists, but also individual portraits, group portraits—including those of children in the classroom—and scenes of purely local interest. This particular scene shows Arena photographing in the midst of ruins, probably the result of the battle for the liberation of Naples from the Bourbon rule in 1861.

There are, in addition, interesting personal glimpses of Arena's professional associations and work as a photographer. One of the prints depicts Arena's studio, complete with ornate velvet chairs, petit-point stools, props, stands, and balustrade, and of course, the camera itself. A camera belonging to Arena, like the one depicted here, is part of the Horblit collection (see case 8)

Case 8

The Studio of Giacomo Arena

Possibly more than any other highlights of this collection, the Giacomo Arena material exemplifies Harrison Horblit's collecting interests. To establish facts on the basis of samples—as many samples as possible—and to establish connections among them is the stuff of scientists. Harrison Horblit was above all a historian of science. The *oeuvre* of Giacomo Arena might not be that of a Daguerre or a Talbot, but it is represented in the Horblit collection by some 68 prints, 215 paper negatives, and photographic apparatus. This body of work yields interesting facts and raises even more interesting questions about Arena's practice, his associations, and the status of commercial photography in southern Italy in the second part of the century. What prompted Harrison Horblit to collect such material was its potential for research. This is also the principle that guided his wife, Jean, in placing the Horblit collection in a research institution for the benefit of students, faculty, and scholars.

37
Giacomo Arena Studio

Portrait of Giacomo Arena, ca. 1860

Albumen silver print; image: 17 x 11.5 cm, mount: 18.7 x 14.2 cm.

Inscribed on the mount, in a contemporary hand: "Giacomo Arena, 1818–1906"

Little is known of Giacomo Arena's early years. Born in 1818, we find him practicing photography in Naples from the 1860s to the 1880s, first at 7, Strada Pace, and later on the Piazza dei Martiri. The branch he opened in Pozzuoli was still active in the early 1900s. By 1867, Arena had made a name for himself and participated in the Paris Universal Exhibition. By the 1870s, he was associated with the Fratelli D'Alessandri of Rome, especially Antonio D'Alessandri, well known for his photographs of Roman nobility and the pontifical court. In 1899, at age 77, Giacomo Arena came to New York City to join his family who ran a photographic studio.

CATALOGUE NO. 37. Giacomo Arena Studio. *Portrait of Giacomo Arena,* ca. 1860. Albumen silver print; image: 17 x 11.5 cm., mount: 18.7 x 14.2 cm.

This portrait of Arena depicts him as a handsome man in his forties who, as a portrait photographer, knows how to present himself to best advantage. He is sitting at an angle, on a camera emblematic of his profession. His legs and feet are tucked away to his left, his left arm rests comfortably on a chair, the hand slightly animated by a raised middle finger. The whole attitude is relaxed, as he looks confidently into the camera, a well-established, middle-aged man with a distinctive black hat. It might be the same hat that Arena is seen wearing in the field (no. 36).

38
Fabricca Oscar Pettazzi, Milan

Wet-Plate Camera, ca. 1860

Walnut square body with internal dark maroon leather bellows; equipped with a four-inch brass lens from the Viennese firm of Voigtländer & Sohn; rack-and-pinion focusing; 27 x 25 cm. (closed) This camera is accompanied by three plate holders of different sizes and a wooden accessory case (33 x 35 cm.) containing two sets of Waterhouse stops and the back plate holder with ground glass

This beautiful wet-plate camera, dating from the early 1860s, belonged to Giacomo Arena. At the top, it bears the plaque of its manufacturer, the Fabricca Pettazzi of Milan. Prevalent from 1855 to the early 1880s, the wet-collodion process spanned most, if not all, of Giacomo Arena's career. Introduced in 1851 by Frederick Scott Archer, it involved pouring collodion, an emulsion made from gun cotton, onto a perfectly clean glass plate and sensitizing it in a bath of silver nitrate solution. The plate, placed in its holder, was then inserted while still wet into the camera—hence the name of the camera—and exposed briefly. Immediately after exposure, the plate was developed in a solution of pyrogallic and acetic acids and fixed.

As in most wet-plate cameras, the ground glass of this one is removable; the plate holder, inserted from the top, runs in grooves in the back of the camera. The focusing range is determined by the extension allowed by the bellows, while the focal length of the lens may be varied with the use of lens diaphragms, or "stops." While a wet-plate camera might have been relatively easy to use in a studio, photographing in the field meant carrying along, besides the camera and its tripod, a colossal amount of equipment: a tent, a box of glass plates, a sensitizing box, assorted chemicals for sensitizing, developing, and fixing the plates, a number of lenses, and a supply of water.

At least two of the prints in the collection show Arena with a wet-plate camera, one taken in the studio (no. 39), and another taken in the field (no. 36).

CATALOGUE NO. 38. *Wet–Plate Camera*, made by Oscar Pettazzi, Milan, ca. 1860. Walnut body with leather bellows and four-inch brass lens; 27 x 25 cm. (closed).

39
Giacomo Arena Studio

Group Portrait of the Arena and D'Alessandri Staff with Implements, 1870

Dated by hand on the mount; image: 39 x 30 cm., mount: 40.3 x 30.8 cm.

In the late 1860s or early 1870s, Giacomo Arena became associated with the Fratelli D'Alessandri of Rome, in particular with Antonio D'Alessandri. The full nature of their association has yet to be determined. Antonio D'Alessandri, a priest, became interested in photography while in Paris in 1851. He opened his first studio in Rome in the mid-1850s and was joined by his brother, Paolo Francesco. Together, they established an extremely successful business that specialized in portraiture of the Roman nobility. The D'Alessandris were named official photographers of the pontifical court of Pius IX and, after 1861, of the Bourbon court in exile in Rome.

CATALOGUE NO. 39.   Studio of Giacomo Arena. *Group Portrait of the Arena and D'Alessandri Staff with Implements*, 1870. Albumen silver print; image: 39 x 30 cm., mount: 40.3 x 30.8 cm.

The brothers had another specialty, costume photography. They established a large catalogue of costumes typical of Rome and its surroundings, many of them colored by hand for the greater enjoyment of their customers. It has been suggested that costume portraiture is an area in which Giacomo Arena and Antonio D'Alessandri collaborated (Becchetti, 1996, p. 16). Their association and the presence of Antonio as a practicing partner in Naples is documented by this remarkable photograph of the studio staff, taken in the garden of 7, via della Pace. The two partners stand in the back, Antonio D'Alessandri on the right, resting his arm on the wet-plate camera, and Giacomo Arena on the left holding a printing frame. In front of them sit two members of the staff, one of whom holds a palette and a retouching box. In the foreground, the youngest member of the group is shown cleaning glass plates, an assortment of which stand next to him on a rack.

Around 1870, Arena began dating on the mounts, by hand, the photographs issued from his studio. This one is no exception. Although the lower left corner of the mount is damaged, the date of 1870 is clearly visible.

Case 9

Getting Acquainted: Personal Travel Albums

The author of an 1844 British travel guide expressed surprise at the wonderful change that "has taken place in the sentiments of [the British] towards foreigners and foreign countries. They now no longer dread communication; but are anxious, on the contrary, to be acquainted with one and to see the other" (*The Traveller's Hand-Book*, p. B). During the nineteenth century, Europeans traveled to northern Africa, the Middle East, and the Orient as never before, and photographs of these foreign lands were much in demand. Not only did the travelers bring cameras with them on their journeys but native artists also learned photography and sold the images to European tourists.

The first photographic travel book may have been *Sun Pictures in Scotland* (1845), Talbot's homage to Sir Walter Scott's home and haunts in Scotland. The book contains 23 salt prints with no text other than an index and captions. Talbot gambled on the appeal of the individual photographs combined with popular sentiment toward Scott, who had recently died. In the same vein, Calvert Jones, Charles Fredricks, Désiré Charnay, and others traveled to foreign places and returned with photographs they hoped would have commercial appeal. As the practice of photography became easier, amateurs joined in, documenting their journeys and saving their photographs in albums, just as they had done with family pictures. Others preferred simply to buy photographs as they traveled, collecting obligatory views of the popular tourist sites, along with images of the curious and exotic. The Horblit collection contains albums dedicated to each of the European countries as well as Russia, Japan, India, and the Middle East. They not only document nineteenth-century life in a variety of cultures but also reflect the widespread use of photography by professionals and amateurs alike.

40

Japanese School

Views of Japan
Unpublished album, 1890s
71 hand-colored albumen silver prints; volume: 28 x 38 cm.

On display: Stone Gate Mitake Koshiw., no. 1056, and Kasuga, Nara, no. 1248

Japan existed in relative isolation for several centuries before Commodore Matthew Perry's fleet landed in Tokyo Bay in 1853. One member of the party was daguerreotypist Eliphalet Brown, Jr. No sooner had the Americans landed and procured a house than Perry ordered Brown to "prepare his materials, occupy the building, and commence the practice of his art" (Hawks, p. 154). Although Brown was not the first photographer to practice in Japan, the arrival of the Americans and the subsequent signing of trade agreements brought an influx of Western practices, influencing the dress, social structure, and arts of the Japanese people. In addition, the use of photography became widespread. The first two professional Japanese photographers, Ueno Hikoma and Shimooka Renjō, both opened their studios in 1862, the same year that the first Japanese book on photography was published. Felice Beato arrived in Japan the following year and formed a commercial press with the artist Charles Wirgman. Together they published a magazine entitled *Japan Punch*, and a later variation, *The Far East*, which they illustrated with original photographs. By 1877, there were over a hundred commercial photographers in Tokyo alone, and in the last two decades of the century a tremendous market emerged for albums of photographs.

All the photographs in this album are unsigned, hand-colored commercial prints. Ukiyo-e woodblock printing was still the most popular visual medium in Japan when photography was introduced, but the woodblock printers gradually found that there was more work in the new photographic studios. Painted photographs were preferred over black-and-white prints, and the technique of hand coloring rose to a level of sophistication not found in other countries. The demand for photographic albums became so great, the work of several photographers was often mixed to fill the albums, making attribution of individual photographs difficult. For example, in 1877, Beato sold his stock of photographs to an Austrian, Baron von Stillfried, who merged it with the work of other photographers. When the baron left Japan in 1885, his stock was spread among three dealers: Kusakabe Kimbei, A. Farsari, and Tamamura Kōzaburō (Winkel, p. 27). In this album, many of the images are framed with a cameo effect typical of Beato. Photographs were often taken outside the studio in a natural setting (like those on display), and Beato is known to have traveled widely in order to capture such scenes. Although attributing these photographs to Beato is purely speculation, we don't need to know the photographer's name to be charmed by them. The pictures of Sika deer and umbrellas, and of the stone gates to hidden mountain shrines, engage us with their insight and curious humor. These photograph albums have lasting appeal, just as Talbot's own 1845 photographs of Scotland captured public attention and continue to do so today.

C ATA L O G U E N O . 4 1.   Abdullah Frères, *Mendicants Turcs* from *Views of Istanbul,* an unpublished album, 1880s–1890s. Albumen silver print; volume: 25.5 x 32 cm.

41
Abdullah Frères, active 1850s–1890s
Views of Istanbul
Unpublished album, 1880s–1890s
30 albumen and gelatin silver prints; volume: 25.5 x 32 cm.

On display: Mendicants Turcs

Istanbul, formerly Constantinople, was the commercial and cultural center of the Ottoman Empire during the nineteenth century. Writers, painters, and photographers were drawn to its exoticism and brought with them the new technologies of the West. European photographers such as James Robertson, Maxime Du Camp, and Carlo Naya worked in the city during the 1840s and 1850s. Also during this period, a German chemist named Rabach moved to Istanbul and opened a daguerreotype studio. Vichen Abdullah, a local painter of miniatures, was hired to work in the studio, and in 1858, together with two of his brothers, Kevork and Hovsep, Vichen bought the business from Rabach. Under their management and artistry, the studio flourished, and in 1863, the Sultan Abdulaziz appointed the Abdullah Frères official court photographers and outstanding artists of the city (titles they had printed on the back of their photographs). The Abdullah Frères achieved international recognition in 1867, when they exhibited their work in the Turkish pavilion of the Paris Exhibition. The business continued until 1899, when it was sold to the brothers' leading competitors, Pascal Sébah and Policarpe Joaillier (see below H10).

This album includes views of the Dolmabahçe Palace, the Galata Bridge, the Topané Mosque, and the interior of the Imperial Tomb, as well as photographs of whirling dervishes, pretzel dealers, men washing at ablution fountains, and preparing for prayers. The photograph on display shows a night watchman (right) and a begging dervish, identified by his kashkul, or beggar's bowl, and patched wool coat. Public begging was forbidden for all but the Bektāshis, who were wandering dervishes. Paradoxically, the word for dervish in Persian is similar to the word for beggar. The tesbeh, or rosary, in his right hand consists of ninety-nine beads, signifying the number of "beautiful names of Allah." In the taybend, or girdle, around his waist would be a stone known as the "stone of contentment," in memory of former dervishes who bound stones close to their stomachs to suppress hunger.

42
British School
Views of Calcutta
Unpublished album, 1890s
20 albumen silver prints, with 5 additional photographs laid inside the cover; volume: 18.5 x 24.7 cm.

On display: Snake Charmers and *Cart Laden with Straw*

CATALOGUE NO. 42.   British School. *Snake Charmers* from *Views of Calcutta*, an unpublished album, 1890s. Albumen silver print; volume: 18.5 x 24.7 cm.

Photography reached Calcutta in 1840, and three years later, Charles Shepherd established the first commercial studio in Simla. It was government and corporate sponsorship, however, not private enterprise, that was primarily responsible for the rapid advancements of photography in India. By the 1850s, the regional governments each had their own royal photographer with commissions for archeological surveys and architectural documentation. The East India Company's Military Department began employing photographers in 1855, and many British officers took pictures on their own, even exhibiting their work in local shows. An 1856 guidebook recommended "to every assistant-surgeon to make himself master of photography in all its branches, on paper, on plate glass, and on metallic plates. . . . During the course of his service in India, he may make such a faithful collection of man and animals, of architecture and landscape, that would be a welcome contribution to any museum" (McCosh, p. 46). Photographic societies were founded in both Bombay and Calcutta, with regular competitions that included European and Indian photographers. While foreign commercial photographers greatly outnumbered the native artists at first, by 1860 there were 130 Bengali photographers registered in Calcutta and fewer than 200 Europeans. Vernacular scenes of Indian life were compiled in the twenty-four volumes of *The Indian Amateurs Photographic Album*, issued between December 1856 and October 1858 and, later, in *The People of India*, an eight-volume work published between 1868 and 1875.

It is not surprising that one of the most elegant albums in the Horblit collection is a late nineteenth-century record of Calcutta, the city whose lively cultural climate had fostered the development of photography in India. This small, brown volume appears to be the work of a single person, who has carefully taken or collected photographs of local scenes. The trimmed, albumen prints are not glued to the pages but carefully inserted under paper strips that loosely hold the corners. In a delicate script, a penciled caption describes the location of each image. The photographs are mostly formal portraits of streets or government buildings, such as Esplanade Row, Old Court House Street, the Town Hall, and the Eden Gardens. A number of views include the Hooghly (or Hugli) River, commercially the most important channel of the Ganges River because it is navigable to Calcutta and the Bay of Bengal. The stillness of these scenes—from the quiet streets to the calm waters—evokes a serenity that is uncharacteristic of the Indian city we know today. The album records a picturesque Victorian Calcutta, with only a few views outside the capital, such as those of traders returning from the market in Darjeeling or a farmer leading his oxen with a wagon of straw. Only one exotic image has been included in the album: a group of snake charmers barely captured in the frame, as though the photographer did not dare hold the camera still at such a scene.

43

Photographer unknown

Views of Portugal, Spain, and Morocco

Unpublished album, 1870s–1880s

90 albumen and gelatin silver prints; volume: 29 x 24.5 cm.

On display: two-plate panorama of Gibraltar from the Devil's Tongue

This album begins in Portugal, with photographs of Lisbon, the Tower on the Tagus, and the Aqueducto das Aguas Livres, then moves to Cintra, now Sintra, celebrated by Lord Byron in *Childe Harold's Pilgrimage.* Next, the photographer crosses the Strait of Gibraltar to Tangier, and we see the outer marketplace, the Great Mosque, and a crowded street where a religious ceremony known as the Progress of the Aysawa is being celebrated. Women look on from one rooftop, Jews from another, and a crowd of Europeans with cameras watch from a third vantage point, while the photographer is perched in the steeple of the Catholic Church. Back in Spain, the album leads us to the bullring in Málaga, cathedrals in Cádiz, and ends with views of Vigo. Interspersed among these images are some photographs of England and northern Wales. They seem to have been placed wherever there were empty pages opposite the Spanish views. Many are gelatin silver prints from a much later date and were probably added by a subsequent owner of the album.

The view on display is a two-plate panorama of the Rock of Gibraltar, known as one of the Pillars of Hercules that marked the very end of the world. The photograph was taken from the two-mile isthmus known as the Devil's Tongue, a mass of masonry lined with cannons on either side. A similar panoramic view was published in J. H. Mann's *A History of Gibraltar and Its Sieges* (1873), also in the Horblit collection. It is a commonly photographed view of this ancient fortress with its English garrison, the prize of nearly 800 years of war between the Spaniards and the Moors. The rock itself is over three miles long, leaving only nine miles separating Europe from Africa. In the late nineteenth century, 5,000 to 6,000 troops were stationed there, and the cannons were fired everyday at sunrise, sunset, and nine o'clock, when the soldiers went to bed. Describing Gibraltar in the eighteenth century, Edmund Burke called it "a post of power, a post of superiority, of connection, of commerce—one which makes us invaluable to our friends and dreadful to our enemies" (Field, p. 120), impressions still conveyed today by this photograph.

Case 10

Medical Research and Photography

The 1860s and 1870s saw the remarkable congruence of medical research and photography. While the medical profession tirelessly observed and described symptoms and attempted to link them to pathologies in an effort to diagnose and treat diseases, photography now made it possible, as no medium had before, to capture symptoms and treatments visually. From the observations of muscular contraction by Duchenne de Boulogne to the surgical studies of Josiah Johnson Hawes and the neurological or mental pathologies recorded by Bourneville and Régnard, photography soon became an integral part of medical research.

During the same period, the rapid development of photomechanical processes—from woodburytypes to collotypes and photolithographs—allowed for greater ease of reproduction, larger print runs, and an increased number of publications. The efflorescence of medical photography was not without excesses and loss of innocence, however. While early evaluations equated photographic capture with objective observation and veracity, later assessments warned of the dangers of posed sessions, subjective interpretation, and excesses of imagination (Darwin, 1872, p. 14).

The history of science was Harrison Horblit's first love and primary interest as a collector, and his collection is particularly rich in the area of scientific and medical photography. As early as 1964, before Horblit had even begun collecting photographs, his Grolier Club exhibition catalogue, *One Hundred Books Famous in Science*, boasted several early works that were related to photography or photographically illustrated. Included in his catalogue and part of his subsequent collection of early photography were François Arago's *Rapport sur le Daguerréotype* and Louis J. M. Daguerre's *Historique et Description des Procédés du Daguerréotype*, both published in 1839.

DUMB-BELL CHARTS IN THE BACKGROUND.

GEORGIE.   EDWIN.   HAMIL.   GRUBB.   ORVILLE.   JAMES.   NEDDIE

ABRAM.

CATALOGUE NO. 44. Frederick Gutekunst. *The Mind Unveiled; or, A Brief History of Twenty-Two Imbecile Children* (Philadelphia: U. Hunt & Son, 1858). Albumen silver print; volume: 19 x 13.5 cm.

44

Frederick Gutekunst, 1831–1917

The Mind Unveiled; or, A Brief History of Twenty-Two Imbecile Children

Text by Isaac Newton Kerlin

Philadelphia: U. Hunt & Son, 1858

Illustrations include 2 albumen silver prints; volume: 19 x 13.5 cm.

On display: untitled group photograph of retarded children, opposite p. [48]; signed in the negative, "Gutekunst, Artist"

   Isaac Newton Kerlin practiced medicine at the Pennsylvania Institute for Feeble Minded Children in Germantown, Pennsylvania, from 1858 to 1893. His published works were among the first analyses of the causes of mental deficiency in children and adults, and his medical career was devoted to their care. *The Mind Unveiled*, published in his first year at the institute, was conceived as an appeal for funds rather than a medical text, "the little narrative [being compiled] with an earnest desire, that its perusal may create a deeper and more active interest in the poor imbecile, who needs protection and demands sympathy" (p. 147).

The book contains two tipped-in photographs, a very early, if not the first, instance of photographic illustration in an American psychiatric or medical publication (Burns, pt. 5, p. 279). They are the work of Frederick Gutekunst, who opened his photography studio at 706 Arch Street in Philadelphia in 1856 and who would become known for his portraits of Civil War generals.

The 1850s were a time of optimism in the treatment of the mentally retarded. It was commonly assumed that proper education could reverse or even cure retardation. Accordingly, the children depicted in this photograph sit against a backdrop of dumbbell charts, surrounded by educational tools—among them blocks, an alphabet, and a blackboard—with a violin in the foreground.

45
Guillaume Benjamin Duchenne de Boulogne, 1806–1875

Mécanisme de la physionomie humaine ou Analyse électro-physiologique de l'expression des passions applicable à la pratique des arts plastique . . . avec un atlas composé de 74 [i.e. 84] figures électro-physiologiques photographiées

Paris: Veuve Jules Renouard, 1862. 2 vols. (vol. 1: text; vol. 2: atlas of plates)
Illustrations in this copy include 85 albumen silver prints (photographic frontispiece in vol. 1 and 84 prints mounted on printed boards in vol. 2); in addition, 3 prints from another copy have been inserted; volume: 28.5 x 19 cm.

On display: Spécimen d'une expérience électro-physiologique faite par l'auteur, frontispiece to vol. 1; Muscle de la douleur, Sourcilier, vol. 2, plate 28.

Guillaume Benjamin Duchenne, surnamed "de Boulogne" for his native Boulogne-sur-Mer, was trained as a medical doctor and studied applied electricity at the Académie de Médecine in Paris, where he began practicing in 1842. Using the technique of *faradisation localisée*—the application of electricity to human musculature—Duchenne developed what amounts to a muscular cartography of the human body, fathering in the process the fields of electrodiagnosis and electrotherapy.

In the early 1850s, Duchenne began to investigate the "grammar and orthography of human facial expression." He established a list of fundamental expressions, seeking through electrical stimulation to tie them directly to the contraction of a particular facial muscle or muscle group. Duchenne considered photography an essential part of his study. He taught himself the new art, and enlisted Adrien Tournachon to help produce the plates for the *Mécanisme de la physionomie humaine*. At least six subjects were experimented upon for the purpose of the study, the most famous of whom was the old, toothless man whose thin, grimacing face has become synonymous with the work of Duchenne.

Duchenne's *Mécanisme*—the first work on physiognomy to be illustrated with photographs—was intended for a scientific as well as an artistic audience. It elicited praise on the part of Darwin, who made use of Duchenne's photographs in *The Expression of the Emotions in Man and Animals* (see no. 46). However, the aesthetic import of the *Mécanisme* failed to be understood as well as Duchenne had hoped. Convinced nevertheless of the artistic potential of his research, Duchenne bequeathed the large original photographs for the book to l'École des Beaux-Arts in Paris.

There are two copies of the first edition of Duchenne's *Mécanisme* in the Horblit collection, with slightly different collations. An extended essay by Robert Sobieszek, entitled "'Gymnastics of the Soul': The Clinical Aesthetics of Duchenne de Boulogne," appears in the companion volume to this catalogue, *Six Exposures: Essays in Celebration of the Opening of the Harrison D. Horblit Collection of Early Photography*.

46

The Expression of the Emotions in Man and Animals, with Photographic and Other Illustrations
Text by Charles Darwin
London: John Murray, 1872
Illustrations include 7 heliotypes from negatives by Guillaume Benjamin Duchenne de Boulogne, Oscar Gustav Rejlander, Kindermann, and Dr. Wallich; volume: 19.6 x 13.7 cm.

On display: Weeping, pl. I

Charles Darwin published *The Expression of the Emotions in Man and Animals* in 1872, five years after *On the Origin of Species*. The new work further substantiated his evolutionary theory by refuting the idea that the facial muscles of expression in man were a special endowment (R. B. Freeman, p. 142).

The photographs for *The Expression* came from various sources. Darwin commissioned some from Oscar Gustav Rejlander; others he borrowed from Duchenne (his "magnificent photographs" for the *Mécanisme de la physionomie humaine*) and from Herr Kindermann of Hamburg and Dr. Wallich, who furnished him with "excellent negatives of crying infants; and . . . a charming one of a smiling girl" (pp. 23–25). A total of seven photographic plates, in addition to twenty-one wood engravings, illustrated the first edition of *The Expression*.

"All these photographs," claimed Darwin, "have been printed by the heliotype process, and the accuracy of the copy is thus guaranteed" (p. 25). Indeed, the photographic illustrations of *The Expression* were among the first successful examples of heliotypes. Invented by Ernest Edwards, the heliotype, a photomechanically produced image, was made by exposing a gelatin film under a negative. The gelatin was then transferred to a plate and, hardened with chrome alum, could be printed directly like a lithograph. The American rights to the process—patented both in England and in America—were purchased by the Boston firm of James R. Osgood & Co., which made the first commercial use of the process in 1872. Eminently suited to publication, heliotypes remained popular on both continents throughout the 1870s.

CATALOGUE NO. 46.   Herr Kindermann (attributed to). *Weeping* from Charles Darwin, *The Expressions of the Emotions in Man and Animals, with Photographic and Other Illustrations* (London: John Murray, 1872) pl. I. Heliotype; volume: 19.6 x 13.7 cm.

47
Valette, J.

Nouveau traité élémentaire et pratique des maladies mentales, suivi de considérations pratiques sur l'administration des asiles d'aliénés . . . avec huit planches en photoglyptie

Text by Henri Dagonet
Paris: J. B. Baillère, 1876
Illustrations include 8 mounted woodburytypes with printed captions: "Clichés J. Valette, Photoglyptie Lemercier et Cie"; volume, 23.8 x 15.2 cm.

On display: Manie, plate I

  Henri Dagonet, son of a prominent medical doctor and mental asylum director, forged his own career as an aliéniste following the defense of a brilliant thesis at the Faculté de Paris in 1849. Dagonet taught psychiatry at the University of Strasbourg and practiced in a mental institution in

Stephansfeld during the 1850s. At the height of his career, in 1867, Dagonet was named medical director of the Asile Saint-Anne in Paris. He devoted the next decade to bettering conditions at the asylum, strengthening the administration, and developing a special course of instruction for psychiatric nurses. The last part of *Nouveau traité* is in fact an administrative manual for mental institutions, the result of Dagonet's comparative research and personal experience.

The main part of the treatise, however, is a nomenclature of the principal types of mental illness, followed by a list of their causes and proposed treatments. Photographs provided a particularly useful accompaniment to this nomenclature, according to Dagonet: "What is new [in this publication] is the addition of photographs representing various types of mentally ill patients: the reader, once he has learned to familiarize himself with their distinctive physiognomies, will be able to establish the diagnosis on his own. We have been fortunate to be able to draw from the [photographic] collections that M. M. [Charles] Hildenbrand and [Jules Bernard] Luys [two medical colleagues] have put to our disposal" (p. iv).

Another novelty in this edition was the use of photoglyptie—actually its first use in medical photography, according to Dagonet. Photoglyptie, or woodburytype, was a photomechanical process patented in 1864 by Walter Bentley Woodbury. It consisted of exposing to light a collodion negative on a gelatin film applied to glass. Hardened by light and separated from the glass, the gelatin relief plate, which varied in thickness according to the tones of the original picture, was pressed into a lead plate to produce one or several intaglio molds. Each mold, filled again and again with pigmented gelatin, could produce as many as 600 impressions. Although woodburytypes were relatively cumbersome and expensive to produce, the continuous tone and remarkable tonal scale, as well as the durability of the plates, made them popular until the turn of the century.

48

Désiré Magloire Bourneville, 1840–1909, and Paul Régnard, 1850–1927
Iconographie photographique de la Salpêtrière (Service de M. Charcot)

Paris: Aux bureaux du Progrès médical, V. A. Delahaye, 1876 [i.e. 1877]–1880. 3 vols.
Each volume illustrated with 1 photograph on the title page and 40 plates after negatives by Paul Régnard (vol. 1: albumen silver prints; vols. 2 and 3: photolithographs); volumes: 24.3 x 19.5 cm.

On display: Attitudes passionnelles, Extase (1878), vol. 2, plate XXIII

Professor Jean Martin Charcot, director of the neurological unit at the Salpêtrière, described the Paris hospital in the 1870s as "a large asylum housing more than 5,000 patients of all ages, many of them incurable, permanent residents suffering from chronic disorders affecting in particular the nervous system" (Charcot, vol. 3, pp. 3–4). The sheer size of this "live pathological museum" made the Salpêtrière a unique resource for observation and the comparative study of clinical "types."

The publications of Charles Darwin and Henri Dagonet had recently demonstrated the medical use of photography. Charcot and his collaborator, Désiré Magloire Bourneville, sought to

CATALOGUE NO. 48.   Désiré Magloire Bourneville and Paul Régnard. *Attitudes passionnelles, Extase* from *Iconographie photographique de la Salpêtrière* (Paris: Aux bureaux du Progrès médical, V. A. Delahaye, 1876 [i.e. 1877]–1880) vol. 2, pl. XXIII. Photolithograph; volume: 24.3 x 19.5 cm.

document photographically the epileptic and hysterical episodes of their patients. Paul Régnard, a gifted young intern who joined the Salpêtrière in 1875, assisted them. For the next four years, Régnard and Bourneville recorded their observations and photographed the passing stages of the *attaques*, some so ephemeral that the naked eye alone could not make them out (Londe, pp. 3–4). They were assisted in their efforts by the creation in 1878 of a photographic laboratory—complete with stage, props, and accessories—annexed to Professor Charcot's neurological unit.

The three volumes of the *Iconographie photographique de la Salpêtrière* are the result of these efforts. The illustrations in the first volume are pasted-in albumen silver prints, while those of volumes two and three were done in photolithography, a process that, in the words of Bourneville, "maintains all the guaranties of veracity inherent to photography, while presenting the advantage of printing with greasy ink" (vol. 2, p. ii).

CASE 11

Fad and Fancy: Photography in Everyday Life

The photographic market in the 1840s was dominated by Daguerre's process of making unique images on silver-coated copper plate, although they required tremendous time, expense, and expertise to produce. In the 1850s and 1860s, efforts to simplify photography so a wider audience could afford and enjoy it resulted in a rapid succession of new processes, each embraced and then discarded as a faster or cheaper method took its place. Beginning with the use of collodion in 1851, entrepreneurs and amateur enthusiasts devised the ambrotypes, tintypes, stereographs, *cartes de visite* and cabinet cards, along with the solar camera to make mammoth enlargements and the multiple-lens camera to create dozens of miniature images. The solemn formality of earlier photographs gave way to livelier, more spontaneous, and even whimsical portraits. A wider range of races and classes began to appear in these images, in rural as well as urban settings, as photography made its way into middle-class lives.

Photographs became a necessary part not only of family ceremonies, such as marriages and graduations, but also of public events. The American Civil War stimulated the rapid growth of the commercial industry as photographers traveled with the troops, supplying portraits and views for the soldiers to send home. Newspapers and magazines found ways to add photographic images to their issues, since their readers wanted to see the actual people and events in the news. Important figures became known, for the first time, by the way they looked rather than by what they said. Celebrities such as Jenny Lind and Tom Thumb posed at many commercial studios, which marketed the portraits to an eager public. In this way, photography flourished in the late nineteenth century, and the world would never again be content without it.

CATALOGUE NO. 49a.   American School. *Portrait of Two Girls and a Young Boy Dressed Identically*, ca. 1890. Hand-painted tintype; image: approximately 23 x 19 cm., frame: 50 x 45 cm.

49a
American School

Portrait of Two Girls and a Young Boy Dressed Identically, **ca. 1890**

Hand-painted tintype in printed mat and oak frame; image: approximately 23 x 19 cm., frame: 50 x 45 cm.

49b
American School

Portrait of an Elderly Man

Tintype; 17.5 x 12.5 cm.

49c
American School

Portrait of Two Men Seated in a Riverside Setting

Tintype; 17 x 10.5 cm.

49d
American School

Portrait of a Woman Standing Beside a Settee

Tintype; 21.3 x 16 cm.

49e
American School

Portrait of a Mother and Father with Seven Daughters

Tintype; 19 x 14.3 cm.

49f
American School

Portrait of an African-American Man

Tintype; 17.5 x 12.5 cm.

49g
American School

Portrait of a Baby Seated on a Table

Tintype; 21.3 x 16 cm.

CATALOGUE NOS. 51a–c. Ambrotype jewelry.

49h
American School

Portrait of a Seated Girl

Tintype, 21.5 x 16.4 cm.

Tintypes can be traced back to A. A. Martin, a Frenchman who wrote about the process in 1853. They were patented three years later by an American, Hamilton L. Smith, who quickly sold the rights to his associate, Peter Neff, Jr. Tintypes, also called ferrotypes, were made from Archer's wet collodion process, usually on a plate of black lacquered iron rather than glass. Like the daguerreotype, the tintype was a unique image, but it was quicker to make (under ten minutes from start to finish), cheaper to buy, lightweight yet more durable than a paper print, and easier to view than the reflective daguerreotype. Tintypes lacked the intrinsic beauty of daguerreotypes but sold by the thousands in the United States. People from all walks of life sat for tintypes, in poses from the formal to the private, from the elaborately designed to the spontaneous. Even in its day, however, the tintype failed to receive the respect accorded other photographic processes. An 1873 ferrotyper's guidebook noted that the tintype "has been much retarded by a jealous feeling among photographers, who have tried to degrade it and to 'kill' it. Just as the telegraph, the railway, the steamboat, and hundreds of other comparatively modern improvements were ridiculed in the beginning, so were ferrotypes hooted at and cried down by photographers" (*The Ferrotyper's Guide*, pp. 4–5).

By the 1860s, multiple-lens cameras could easily produce a dozen gem tintypes at a time, each the size of a postage stamp. Some were used for jewelry, but more often, they were placed in small, embossed albums with locket-style clasps and double-sided paper mats (there are five such albums in the Horblit collection). Large-format tintypes were heavily painted in oil—bright colors were favored—to compensate for the lack of tone, often completely obscuring the original image. The images were placed in elaborate printed mats and gilded wood frames to embellish the portraits. In the 1859 manual *How to Colour a Photograph*, the reader is reminded that color is "the sunshine of art, that clothes poverty in smiles, and renders the prospect of barrenness itself agreeable, while it heightens the interest, and doubles the charms of beauty" (preface). The Horblit collection includes 79 individual tintypes, from gem size to mammoth plates.

50
American School

Marriage Certificate with Portraits of George P. Heath and Carrie R. Susley, December 22, 1891

Printed marriage certificate with two tintypes inserted; image: approximately 10 x 6 cm., frame: 52 x 38 cm.

Crider and Brothers was a publishing house in York, Pennsylvania, during the 1860s. Henry M. Crider had the idea of making printed, poster-size marriage certificates into which photographs of the bride and groom (and sometimes the minister) could be inserted. Similar plates

CATALOGUE NO. 50. American School. *Marriage Certificate with Portraits of George P. Heath and Carrie R. Susley, December 22, 1891.* Printed marriage certificate with two tintypes inserted; images: approximately 10 x 6 cm., frame: 52 x 38 cm.

were created to display a family genealogy or postmortem photographs, and they remained popular in the northeastern states until the turn of the century. This particular Crider marriage certificate was copyrighted in 1890 and used by a Maryland couple the following year. It has been placed in a simple, flat-speckled frame that was common in the late 1880s.

51a
American School
Portrait of a Man
Brooch with hand-colored ambrotype; brooch: 5 x 4.5 cm.

51b
American School
Portrait of a Man
Metal swivel brooch with hand-colored ambrotype and locks of hair behind image; brooch: 6 x 5.4 cm.

51c
American School
Portrait of a Man and Portrait of a Woman
Metal swivel brooch with ambrotype and hand-colored albumen print; brooch: 7 x 6 cm.

51d
American School
Portrait of a Seated Woman
Pendant with hand-colored daguerreotype; pendant: 7.2 x 5 cm.

Beginning in the 1840s, daguerreotype jewelry was a novelty item created and collected in both Europe and the United States. The less expensive ambrotypes, another variation of Archer's wet collodion process, and lightweight tintypes also found their way into pendants, earrings, buttons, stickpins, rings, and watch keywinds. Campaign buttons with photographic portraits were first used during the 1860 presidential race between Abraham Lincoln and Stephen A. Douglas. The British market for such keepsakes exploded after Prince Albert's death in 1861, when Queen Victoria and her family began to wear jewelry with photographic miniatures of the late Prince Consort.

The Horblit collection has a total of 25 pieces of jewelry (pendants, lockets, and brooches) containing original photographs, all of which are portraits. The images are in a variety of media, including daguerreotypes, ambrotypes, tintypes, and penny (paper) prints, and several have two different formats in one piece. Only three are portraits of women alone; the rest are pictures of men or family groups, presumably meant for a wife or mother to wear. Several lockets also contain a poem or human hair along with the photograph.

52

Photographer unknown

Family scrapbook

Unpublished album, ca. 1910

Illustrations include 71 albumen and gelatin silver prints; volume: 29.5 x 22.6 cm.

On display: four photographs of bicycles

Small, mounted photographs known as *cartes de visite* were introduced by a Parisian photographer, André Disdéri, who developed a method for producing multiple views on a single sheet, thus greatly reducing production costs. He patented the process late in 1854. *Cartes de visite* and the larger-format cabinet cards became enormously popular and were bought and sold by the dozens. Collecting and trading images, particularly portraits of local celebrities and royalty, was a popular pastime. The Horblit collection includes seven small albums designed specifically to hold these cards, as well as several larger albums, such as the one displayed, which include *cartes de visite* and other photographic formats.

This album begins, as was the custom, with a photograph of a public figure (Queen Victoria) admired by the owner. Along with personal photographs, the album contains commercial prints by William Bambridge, Whitby, Folkestone, W. W. Winter, Lock & Whitfield, Samuel Robert, Robert Bull, and Bradshaw & Godart. The photographs date from 1862 to the early twentieth century.

On display are four photographs of nineteenth-century bicycles, evidence of the rapid changes in popular culture at this time. On the left page, at the bottom left, is the Ordinary or High bicycle, developed in the 1870s, and later called the Penny Farthing. The Coventry Lever Tricycle, later the Salvo quadricycle, is shown at the bottom right, and the Dublin tricycle is above it. Tricycles or quadricycles were easier to ride for women in long skirts and briefly replaced the two-wheel bicycle. When Queen Victoria purchased two Salvos, in 1881, the bicycle became known as the Royal Salvo. On the right page is the Sociable, a tricycle designed for two riders side by side; the riders here are identified only as Aunt Sally and Aunt Hannah. Although women commonly rode in the public parks, they would be reprimanded if their skirts were not long enough to cover their feet and ankles. In the 1880s, a bicycle was marketed specifically for photographers; with a space for a large box camera and several storage boxes for plates and chemicals. This bicycle, like many nineteenth-century fads, quickly came and went.

CASE 12

Private and Personal: Family Albums

The spread of commercial photography in the nineteenth century can be traced through advertisements and business listings, but the extent to which photography was practiced as a hobby is difficult to estimate. Amateur clubs were organized throughout Great Britain, but there were few in the rest of Europe. Distinguished figures such as Prince Albert and Lewis Carroll are well known for their devotion to photography. Ordinary people also taught themselves to use a camera, practicing on family members and friends, and thanks primarily to these amateurs, photography quickly became an integral part of important family events such as weddings, deaths, and trips away from home.

There were no shortcuts for these amateurs. Early photographic processes were difficult to master, the equipment was expensive, the chemistry was uncertain, and the photographer's fingers were conspicuously stained black by silver nitrate. Yet, thousands of people around the world succeeded in mastering the art. We know this because so many photographs survive, lovingly mounted in albums or scrapbooks and accompanied, if we are lucky, by detailed captions identifying the people and places portrayed.

The Horblit collection contains 120 unpublished albums, scrapbooks, and diaries with original photographs dating from the 1840s through the turn of the century. These albums show us not only what people chose to photograph but what they chose to preserve. Technically, the photographs may not represent great achievements (although there are surprises in a few albums), but they offer a history of nineteenth-century family life and travel as well as a record of the development of photography outside the commercial market. Five British albums have been chosen for this exhibition.

CATALOGUE NO. 53.   Benjamin Browning. *At St. George's Bay, Hauraki [Gulf], New Zealand (Anna Churtore & Harriette Dyer)*, 1859, from the Browning-Dansey unpublished album, (1847–1868). Albumen silver print; volume: 20.5 x 17.3 cm.

53
Benjamin Browning, active 1850s–1880s, and George Dansey, active 1850s–1860s

Browning-Dansey Album

Unpublished album, 1847–1868
Illustrations include 109 salted paper and albumen silver prints; volume: 20.5 x 17.3 cm.

On display: B. B. & Mrs. F. B., June 1863, attributed to George Dansey, and *At St. George's Bay, Hauraki [Gulf], New Zealand (Anna Churtore & Harriette Dyer)*, by Benjamin Browning, 1859

This album begins with three photographs: a small family house, an older woman with a young man, and a gypsy caravan. The gypsies are never explained, but we find out later that the man is the B. B., or Benjamin Browning, credited with most of the photographs in the album.

Several prints from paper negatives possibly date as early as 1847. From 1851 to 1868, the prints are captioned and dated in a single hand. They have been pasted into the album in random order, making the family history difficult to decipher. Attribution is also difficult in many cases, because a second photographer, George Dansey, was working in conjunction with Browning. Some photographs have been attributed to one photographer and some to both, while others still bear a combination of names, dates, and initials. One print at the album's center is given two dates, revealing that Dansey made the negative in 1856 and Browning made the print in 1868. This distinction may apply to other prints, although it is clearly indicated only on this one. In several cases, the caption includes "fecit" after Browning's name to clarify the attribution of the photograph.

Browning appears as a young man, often posing with family members. The earliest photographs are images of Dartmouth, Stoke, and other sections of Great Britain, including a visit to London for the Great Exhibition of 1851. A dramatic change takes place in the lives of the Brownings in 1858, as the setting suddenly shifts to Australia and then New Zealand. They visit the Australian Museum and a wool warehouse in Sydney. Large group portraits are taken in Edgecumbe (labeled Mt. Edgecumbe), near Auckland. Browning and others (possibly Dansey) travel to Gibraltar in 1861 and Rome the following year. Someone has pressed flowers near the photographs of these trips. By 1863, the photographs are all of naval barracks and sailing ships, in particular the H. M. S. *Achilles,* and one can assume that Browning has enlisted in military service. As late as 1864, family members are still in New Zealand, leading us to conclude that they were not simply vacationing but settled there in the 1850s. Only one personal comment has been added to help interpret the album. In tiny letters to the side of the photograph on display, the writer has further identified the two women as "Beauty and the Beast."

54
Reverend George Johnston, active 1860s

Jane Charlotte Leathes Album

Unpublished album, 1860–1866
Illustrations include 81 albumen silver prints; volume: 24 x 19 cm.

On display: Miss Johnston 1866 and eleven photographs *By the Rev. G. Johnston 1862;* titles from penciled inscriptions

The provenance of this album is clear. Stamped on the cover is the name of the owner, Jane Charlotte Leathes, and an inscription reads, "J. C. Leathes from her Mother, Oct. 1860—Photographs." The photographer is even credited at the top of several pages: "By Rev. G. Johnston." Pasted on the back of the front cover is the photograph of a memorial plaque inscribed, "In memory of Henry Mussenden Leathes Esq. Lord of the Manors of Herringfleet and Reedham, late of the Royal Horse Artillery, the Waterloo, and Peninsular campaigns, aged 76 years." The young age of Jane in these photographs suggests that Henry Leathes may have been her grandfather.

Jane and her mother lived in Broughton, England, and the photographs collected in this album date from 1860 to 1866. The majority are tiny pictures known as penny prints, from 4 to 7 cm. high, with as many as twelve pasted on a page. Besides portraits of both Jane and Reverend Johnston, there are portraits of Misses Edith and Annie Johnston, who appear to be the reverend's sisters. Throughout the album the women are seen in careful poses with hoop skirts, lace shawls, and jewelry, while the men allow themselves to be captured in less formal poses and attire. There are photographs of garden parties, cricket players, and hunters, but the key event in the album is a wedding. The eight bridesmaids and groomsmen have been photographed in pairs, which are numbered and labeled "as we belong!!!" Jane is at the top, number one, paired with a nonchalant Charles Perring, who wears thick mutton chops. The implication, however, is that Jane had more of a future with Reverend Johnston, since the volume ends with a self-portrait of Johnston, taken in 1862. He is shown straddling a chair inside a greenhouse or solarium, clearly at ease with the place. The light streams in from windows behind him as he looks directly into the camera. It is the kind of picture a young girl might stare back at for many years.

55
British School

Merriman Album

Unpublished album, 1852
139 salted paper prints; volume: 27 x 21.7 cm.

On display: Aunt Georgie, Uncle Lendon, Uncle Harvey, Henry & Will Merriman

This album showcases the extended Merriman family, visitors to their home, and the household staff. The title page, with a portrait of James Nathaniel Merriman, is ornately decorated with a gilt border and the inscription, "From EMILY to J.N.M., 21st SEPTEMBER, 1852." Merriman was the son of surgeon John Merriman and, along with his brother, served as Apothecary Extraordinary to Queen Victoria. Inside the album, the photographs are pasted several to a page and captioned in pencil, with inked frames around the images in the first half of the volume. All the photographs are portraits, but the identity of the photographer is never made clear. In each photograph, two or three people are posed outdoors with a screen, carpet, table, and armchairs to create the appearance of a room. Some of the sitters have their pets with them, some have placed props on the table, and a few gentlemen pose in full military uniform. An extended essay about this album, written by John Szarkowski, appears in the companion volume to this catalogue, *Six Exposures: Essays in Celebration of the Opening of the Harrison D. Horblit Collection of Early Photography*.

CATALOGUE NO. 54. Reverend George Johnston. Page of eleven photographs from the Jane Charlotte Leathes unpublished album, 1860–1866. Albumen silver prints; volume: 24 x 19 cm.

56
British School

Annie Herbert Album

Unpublished album, 1878
29 albumen silver prints, volume: 24 x 19 cm.

On display: Raglan Castle, Grand Staircase

This small, red leather album has been covered with a handmade linen slipcase, and the frontispiece is inscribed, "Annie Herbert, Nuneaton, October 19th 1878." The album is filled with pink, yellow, and green pages lined with geometric borders of blue and pink. Throughout the volume are poems and essays interspersed with pastoral photographs of castles, lakes, and forests. The first entry, "Composed in the old Home for Annie Herbert by Geo. J. Williams, October 18th, 1878," appears to have been written earlier and transcribed here by Annie herself. Subsequent entries are copied in the same delicate hand from a variety of sources, including well-known authors such as Tennyson and Owen Meredith (E. R. Bulwer-Lytton) and family friends listed only as "Old Iron" or "L. E. M."

Although Annie was from Nuneaton, a small town in central England, her longest entry tells the legend of Raglan Castle, a fifteenth-century structure in southeast Wales. She has illustrated it with a photograph of the castle in ruins, barely visible through an overgrowth of bushes and vines. Raglan was the castle of the Somersets, earls of Worcester, and the last of the great aristocratic homes to fall during the English civil wars of the 1640s. Reputed to be the richest man in England, Edward Somerset was a scholarly eccentric, not unlike Sir Thomas Phillipps. Somerset owned an immense library as well as a magnificent collection of works of art. There is little actual history in Annie's romantic narrative, just as the castle today, cleared of its thick nineteenth-century foliage, bears little resemblance to her photograph. Except for a few commercial prints, the other photographs in the album are not captioned, suggesting that it served as a kind of memory book for Annie where she could gather her favorite passages and images to enjoy over time.

57
British School

Family Scrapbook of Great Britain, France, and Tibet

Unpublished album, 1862–1875

Illustrations include 100 albumen silver prints; volume: 47 x 27 cm.

On display: double spread of six photographs

This scrapbook, carefully assembled with detailed captions, follows the travels of an unidentified photographer through Europe to Tibet and back to the Isle of Wight. Greeting cards, commercial prints, and personal photographs are included, dating from the 1860s and 1870s. The album begins without a title or inscription but with two photographs recording the wreck of the Mistletoe Yacht, which occurred in 1875. A long section of commercial prints from the

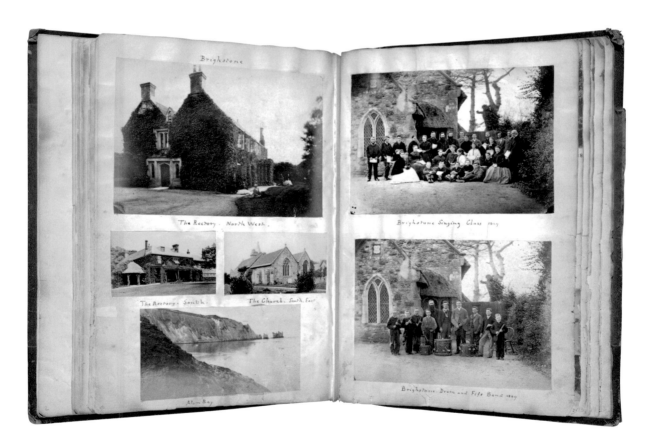

CATALOGUE NO. 57.   British School. Double spread of six photographs, from the *Family Scrapbook of Great Britain, France, and Tibet*, unpublished album, 1862–1875. Albumen silver prints; volume: 47 x 27 cm.

1860s showing tourist sites around Europe is followed by eight small photographs taken in the Himalayas, each dated 1871. The images include a precarious bridge over the Sutlej River (in southwestern Tibet) and the guard's hut at a small, perhaps military, encampment. There are portraits of government and military officials throughout the album, including Lord Palmerston (Henry John Temple, British prime minister from 1855 through 1865), Robert Jamieson and Captain George Huddleston (members of the 11th and 13th Hussars, respectively), Major Carmichael Smyth, Lord and Lady Henry Paulet, and the crew of the H. M. S. *Ariadne*. Several pages of photographs are titled with a general location: Rouen, 1869; Bath, 1874; St.-Ouen, 1869.

On display are some of the many photographs of Brighstone (Isle of Wight) in 1869. Other Isle of Wight tourist attractions depicted are the Blackgang Chine, a notorious haunt for smugglers and ship wreckers in the early nineteenth century; Alum Bay, with its rock formations known as the Needles; and Shanklin Chine. Shanklin was one of many small fishing villages transformed into seaside resorts when the railroad reached them in 1864. The island became popular when Queen Victoria bought an estate there in 1845 for summer holidays. Alfred, Lord Tennyson lived on the island beginning in 1852, as did Julia Margaret Cameron during the 1860s. For a while, the Isle of Wight was the most fashionable resort in Great Britain. In fact, Shanklin became so crowded during the summer that a guidebook complained that "trippers come more often than is desirable, [the island's] beauties are shorn, its glories departed" (Couling, p. 20). Amateur photographers filled the island through the turn of the century.

Case 13

"Permanent" Photographic Processes and the Book

"Beautiful, interesting, and in some respects invaluable as are the productions of photography, there is one fatal drawback to their value—namely, that their continuance cannot be depended upon. . . . What the sun gives, the sun will take away, and there seems to have been no certain means devised under the ordinary process to avert this cruel destiny" (*Illustrated London News*, October 15, 1859, p. 359 [Annan, p. x]). From the very beginning, this cruel destiny was the cause of constant experimentation with new processes that would provide longer-lasting prints. From the carbon printing processes developed in the 1850s and patented by Joseph Swan in 1864 to the photogravure process of Karel Václav Klič, sold throughout European cities by the 1880s, photography achieved major steps toward permanence, hence toward practical commercial applications.

Printing was one of the main industries to benefit from this progress. Whereas albumen prints proved a poor medium for illustration because they lacked permanence and could not be uniformly produced, the new photomechanical processes were well suited to small or deluxe editions. As a result, the last three decades of the century saw the production of a remarkable number of albums and books illustrated with "permanent photographs," both in Europe and in America.

The Horblit collection is strong in such material, with 370 albums and books illustrated with photographs. They complement an already large number of photographically illustrated books in other collections at Harvard, providing a valuable resource for research. Possibly more than any other medium, such illustrated books document the taste, mores, and art of the period, as well as its scenery, changing urban landscape, and associated social concerns.

Catalogue no. 58. Thomas Annan. *Close No. 118, High Street, 1868* from *The Old Closes & Streets of Glasgow, Engraved by Thomas Annan from Photographs Taken for the City of Glasgow Improvement Trust* (Glasgow: James Maclehose and Sons, 1900). Photogravure; volume: 40 x 30 cm.

58
Thomas Annan, 1829–1887

The Old Closes & Streets of Glasgow, Engraved by Thomas Annan from Photographs Taken for the City of Glasgow Improvement Trust, with an Introduction by William Young, R. S. W.

Glasgow: James Maclehose and Sons, 1900
50 photogravures by James Craig Annan from negatives by Thomas Annan; volume: 40 x 30 cm.
One of two issues limited to 100 copies each

On display: Close No. 118, High Street, 1868

Thomas Annan established himself in the 1850s as a practitioner of high-quality art reproduction and architectural and portrait photography in his native city of Glasgow. His early training as a copper plate engraver and his technical bent led him to pioneer two permanent photographic processes. In 1866, Annan acquired from Joseph Swan of Newcastle-on-Tyne the right to practice carbon printing in Scotland, setting up his own carbon printing studio after Swan's patent had lapsed in 1878. Carbon printing did not employ silver but instead was based on the light-sensitive properties of potassium bichromate. At about the same time, Karel Klič, a photographer practicing in Vienna, was experimenting with these properties and perfected what came to be known as the photogravure process. With his son James Craig, Annan went to Vienna in 1883 to learn the new technique directly from its inventor and to secure the rights to the invention for Great Britain and Ireland.

While this experimentation was taking place, Glasgow was grappling with the squalor and unsanitary conditions of its inner city, swelled beyond limits by an unstoppable influx of workers from rural areas who were attracted to its mills and factories. The City Improvement Act of 1866 ordered the demolition and reconstruction of 88 acres of inner-city slums. Annan was commissioned to record for posterity the dilapidated buildings and narrow passageways about to disappear. The series of photographs that resulted—a unique and powerful documentation of the slum conditions of Victorian Glasgow—were published from 1871 to 1900 in a succession of editions reflecting Annan's involvement with permanent processes. While the first edition of 1871 contained 31 pasted-in albumen prints that were relatively sharp but light in tone, the second included 40 carbon plates, rich in deep shadows and sharp contrasts that added a somber touch to an already dark subject. This edition, the third, published posthumously in 1900, contains 50 of Annan's photographs printed in photogravure by James Craig Annan. Lighter in tone than the carbon prints, they have been heavily retouched to eliminate ghosts and add details. They are accompanied, for the first time in this edition, by a letterpress introduction.

CATALOGUE NO. 59.   Peter Henry Emerson. *The Ferry* from *Wild Life on a Tidal Water: The Adventures of a House-Boat and Her Crew* (London: Sampson Low, Marston, Searle, and Rivington, 1890) pl. XXVI. Photogravure; volume: 30 x 25.5 cm.

59
Peter Henry Emerson, 1856–1936

Wild Life on a Tidal Water: The Adventures of a House-Boat and Her Crew

London: Sampson Low, Marston, Searle, and Rivington, 1890

29 photogravures after negatives by P. H. Emerson and 1 after a painting by T. F. Goodall; plates photo-etched by A. Dawson and W. L. Colls; volume: 30 x 25.5 cm.

No. 33 of the deluxe edition limited to 100 copies; there were also 300 copies in the regular edition

On display: The Ferry, plate XXVI

Peter Henry Emerson is best remembered for promoting photography as an independent art and formulating a new aesthetic for it. Emerson publicly denounced the formalism prevalent in England at the time, which reduced photography to a mere imitation of genre painting, complete with staged scenes, professional models, and composition prints. Truthfulness to nature was the basis for Emerson's work and for his friendship and collaboration with T. F. Goodall, the naturalist painter whom he met as he traveled on the Norfolk Broads in 1885. The two friends published *Life and Landscape on the Norfolk Broads* in 1886, meticulously illustrated with platinotypes. The work met with immediate success and prompted Emerson to abandon his medical career and devote himself entirely to photography.

They spent the following summer aboard Goodall's houseboat moored on Breydon Water, photographing the Broads during the day, and at night transcribing the descriptions they had made on the spot. *Wild Life on a Tidal Water* is the fruit of this direct approach to subject matter, both visually and verbally. It is also the result of Emerson's understanding of the advantages of photogravure for book illustration, with its subtle tonal gradations and delicate impressions providing a perfect complement to typography. Emerson's naturalistic aesthetic led him, however, to denounce any kind of corrective handiwork in the photogravure process. For *Wild Life*, he carefully selected Dawson and Colls as the least interventionist practitioners of photogravure.

Later, in a manifesto entitled *The Death of Naturalistic Photography*, published in 1899, Emerson felt compelled to rescind his philosophy and to deny, on technical grounds, the status of art to photography. By that time, however, his earlier views had already altered the course of photography.

60

Richard Hoe Lawrence, active 1880–1890, and others

The Alhambra

Text by Washington Irving, author's revised edition
New York: G.P. Putnam's Sons, Knickerbocker Press, 1891. 2 vols.
31 plates photo-engraved from negatives by Richard Hoe Lawrence and others; volume: 22.5 x 15.5 cm.
No. 64 of the Darro edition, limited to 100 copies, with proofs of the plates on Japanese paper

On display: Entrance to the Mosque of the Alhambra, frontispiece to vol. 1

Richard Hoe Lawrence, gentleman banker, perhaps best exemplifies the role of clubman in turn-of-the-century New York. An active bibliophile, supporter of the arts, and amateur photographer, Lawrence was elected chairman of the Lantern Slide Committee and treasurer of the Society of Amateur Photographers of New York in 1888. He and fellow amateur photographers Henry G. Piffard, consulting surgeon at New York City Hospital, and Dr. John Nagle of the New York City Health Department joined Jacob Riis in the late fall of 1887 in nocturnal photographic forays through the tenements of the Lower East Side. The Richard Hoe Lawrence collection held by the New York Historical Society contains copy prints from Lawrence's lantern slides, donated by his widow to the society in 1950. They reveal that some photographs attributed to Riis are actually Lawrence's uncredited work (Strange, pp. 5–12).

With his great interest in photography and plenty of time on his hands, Lawrence was the perfect choice for the illustration of the deluxe, Darro edition of Washington Irving's *The Alhambra*. Lawrence and others, who remain unidentified, followed in the steps of Washington Irving at the Alhambra some 70 years later. Like Irving but through photography, they sought to depict "its half Spanish, half Oriental character; its mixture of the heroic, the poetic, and the grotesque; to revive the traces of grace and beauty fast fading from its walls" (*The Alhambra*, vol. 1, p. vii). The proofs from their lantern slides, photo-engraved on the finest Japanese paper and accompanied by guardsheets with descriptive letterpress, demonstrate the status and degree of refinement that photogravure had attained. It was considered the perfect match for the elegant typography and ornate gold and maroon moresque borders of this deluxe edition.

61

Herbert Wendell Gleason, 1855–1937

Walden, or Life in the Woods

Text by Henry David Thoreau
Boston: The Bibliophile Society, 1909. 2 vols.
Illustrations include 9 platinum prints by Gleason; volume: 24 x 17.2 cm.
Edition limited to 483 copies printed for members only, most on handmade Holland paper, a few on Japanese vellum; this copy is on Holland paper

On display: White Pond–Blue Flag along Shore, facing p. 62, vol. 2.

The Reverend Herbert Wendell Gleason resigned his ministry at age forty-four, devoting the rest of his life to photography, nature, and conservation. He visited and photographed some of the wildest areas of North America, returning always to the scenery of his native New England. In the early 1900s, Houghton Mifflin commissioned Gleason to illustrate its edition of *The Writings of Henry David Thoreau*. The twenty-volume set, accompanied by more than 100 of Gleason's photographs, was published in 1906. In Thoreau, Gleason found the deepest affinity for his own philosophy and aesthetic. For more than twenty years, he followed in the author's footsteps, identifying the locations he had visited and seeking, through photography, a visual equivalent of Thoreau's imagery.

In 1909, Gleason was commissioned to illustrate a new and limited edition of *Walden* for the members of the Bibliophile Society of Boston. Nine platinum prints were made from Gleason's negatives, mounted on Holland paper, and accompanied by guardsheets printed letterpress with quotations from Thoreau. Invented in 1873 by William Willis, the platinum process was based upon the light sensitivity of iron salts with the final image being metallic platinum. Continually refined, it remained popular until the early decades of the twentieth century, valued especially for its permanence and exceptional tonal range.

Here, as in the earlier edition, Gleason's appreciation of nature is devoid of any affectation. Artistic considerations were, in his own words "wholly secondary" (*Walden*, p. ix). What he sought and obtained was a direct, loving, yet respectful gaze upon nature. It is precisely this quality that grants Gleason's photographs a timeless appeal, whether they illustrate the editions of his time or publications occasioned by the posthumous discovery of thousands of his glass plate negatives (e.g., *The Illustrated Walden*, 1973, and *The Illustrated A Week on the Concord and Merrimack Rivers*, 1983).

CATALOGUE NO. 61.   Herbert Wendell Gleason. *White Pond–Blue Flag along Shore* from Henry David Thoreau. *Walden, or Life in the Woods* (Boston: The Bibliophile Society, 1909) vol. 2, facing p. 62. Platinum print; volume: 24 x 17.2 cm.

Catalogue no. H1.　Frédéric A. Flachéron. *North West Corner of the Roman Forum, with the Temple of Vespasian in the Foreground,* 1850. Salted paper print from a paper negative; image: 33.9 x 25.2 cm., mount: 51.4 x 38.5 cm.

H1

Frédéric A. Flachéron, 1813–1883

North West Corner of the Roman Forum, with the Temple of Vespasian in the Foreground,
Rome, 1850

Salted paper print from a paper negative, signed and dated in the negative; image: 33.9 x 25.2 cm., mount: 51.4 x 38.5 cm.

The excavation and identification of the monuments of the Roman Forum, interrupted in 1834, resumed in the late 1840s under the direction of the architect and archaeologist Luigi Canina. It was during that time that a small group of amateur photographers, known as the Roman Circle, was active in the Eternal City (see case 7). Among them was Count Frédéric A. Flachéron, trained as a sculptor and as a painter, who devoted himself to photography roughly from 1848 to 1853. Attracted by the site, Flachéron photographed the Roman Forum repeatedly during that period.

This northwest view, taken in 1850, shows the Arch of Septimius Severus on the right and three tall Corinthian columns in the foreground. Luigi Canina correctly identified these fluted pillars as remnants of the Temple of Vespasian, formerly known as the Temple of Jupiter Tonans. The construction of the temple was undertaken in 79 A.D. by Vespasian's sons, Titus and Domitian. In the background, overlooking the Forum, stands the church of Santa Martina e San Luca. It is there, in the upper portion of the church, that Canina was laid to rest, in close proximity to his archaeological finds.

The Horblit collection includes another view of the north side of the Forum, which Horblit acquired at the 1987 Vendôme sale as part of a group of 37 Flachéron paper negatives. The negative, dated 1851, is numbered 6 and signed. The horizontal view includes at right the seven granite columns formerly known as the Temple of Concordia. Canina completed the excavation in 1850 and identified it as the Temple of Saturn.

H2

Robert Macpherson, 1811–1872

The Ravine with the Temple of the Sibyl and the Grotto of Neptune, Tivoli, ca. 1863

Albumen silver print; image: 40.3 x 29.8 cm., mount: 63.5 x 47.6 cm.
Macpherson's blind stamp on the recto of the mount, with "122" penciled in the center

With long, flowing red hair, the Scottish kilt of his homeland, and a loud, impassioned manner, Robert Macpherson had a presence that was as powerful and charismatic as his photographs. Originally an Edinburgh surgeon, Macpherson moved to Rome in the 1840s to pursue a career as a painter but after ten years, he still had not found the means to support his new wife and baby. When he was introduced to photography, around 1851, "he threw aside his pencils, which seemed to promise nothing but poverty and disappointment" (J. E. Freeman, p. 204) and quickly established a commercial studio. His architectural views of Rome and its environs, made from 18 x 22" glass plate negatives, were greeted enthusiastically by the tourists and admired by the photographic community back in Scotland. During this period a number of commercial photographers including the Fratelli Alinari, James Anderson, Gioacchino Altobelli, and Tommaso Cuccioni established studios in Rome to sell almost identical views. It was Macpherson, however, who was singled out in John Murray's 1856 *Handbook for Travellers,* the essential guide for English-speaking tourists. "Photography has been of late years, very successfully applied in delineating the monuments of ancient and modern Rome," writes Murray. "By far the finest are those made by our countryman Mr. Macpherson" (Murray, p. xv).

Macpherson was one of Horblit's favorite photographers, and he attempted to collect the artist's entire *oeuvre.* Horblit succeeded in gathering nearly 200 large-format photographs, several versions of Macpherson's broadside, *Photographs of Rome* (a list of photographs available to order), and a copy of his oversize album, *Vatican Sculptures.* The Houghton Library owns a second copy of *Vatican Sculptures,* inscribed to Herman Melville by the author.

Tivoli, known as Tibur until the eighth century, was the favorite retreat of Augustus, Hadrian, and Horace, who mentioned it as the heavenly spot where he hoped to end his days. The Villa d'Este, Hadrian's Villa, and the beautiful Hellenistic Temple of the Sibyl (or Vesta) were, and still are, an obligatory trip for any tourist making the grand tour. Shortly before Macpherson arrived in Rome the Anio River was diverted away from Tivoli because flooding endangered the temple and other landmarks. The small, circular Temple of the Sibyl stands at the edge of a precipice where the water used to fall. In the chasm beneath the temple are the Grottoes of Neptune and the Sirens, once under water, now accessible through winding paths along the cliff. Cardinal Wiseman, archbishop of Westminster, called the Temple of the Sibyl "that most exquisite specimen of art crowning nature, in perfect harmony of beauties" (Hare, p. 670). Throughout history, this little temple has inspired the work of many artists and writers such as Giovanni Piranesi, George Sand, J. M. W. Turner, and John Ruskin, as well as John Soane, who recreated the temple in the middle of London.

CATALOGUE NO. H2. Robert Macpherson. *The Ravine with the Temple of the Sibyl and the Grotto of Neptune,* Tivoli, ca. 1863. Albumen silver print; image: 40.3 x 29.8 cm., mount: 63.5 x 47.6 cm.

H3
Lord William Campbell of Stracathro (attributed to)
Tullichewan Castle, Scotland, ca. 1857

Salted paper print; image: 21.3 x 28.6 cm., mount: 35.6 x 46.7 cm.

It is difficult to attribute a photograph when the photographer is identified only by a common surname. Campbell is a name with a long history in Scotland, not to mention British history in general. In the nineteenth century, there were several prominent photographers named Campbell —Rinhart lists four working in the United States as daguerreotypists, *Craig's Daguerreian Registry* lists fourteen American daguerreotypists, and the *Index to American Photographic Collections* offers eighty-four. The closest match for the Campbell photographers in the Horblit collection is W. G. Campbell, one of the original members of the Photographic Exchange Club and active in London during the 1850s.

The Horblit collection holds three photographs by Campbell. The estate that appears in each has been identified as Tullichewan Castle, Scotland. Colnaghi's *Photography: The First Eighty Years* attributes photographs of Tullichewan not to any of the professional photographers listed above but to an amateur photographer, William Campbell of Strachathro [sic] (p. 78). A member of Scotland's upper class, Lord Campbell is listed in *Burke's Peerage* from 1850 to 1926, and according to Colnaghi, his brother, Sir James Campbell, served as Lord Provost of Glasgow in the 1840s. William was the first Campbell to reside in Tullichewan Castle, which was built in the eighteenth century as a country retreat on the southern banks of Loch Lomond for John Stirling, of the famous Glasgow firm, William Stirling and Sons. Each of the three prints in the Horblit collection depicts the Campbell family, friends, or staff outside the castle, posing casually. A child plays in a wheelbarrow, and one man is identified simply as "Johnnie." These salted paper prints were once part of an album, now disassembled, bearing the following dedication on its cover: "Presented to Miss Campbell by her Uncle, Glasgow, 27th July, 1857."

CATALOGUE NO. H3.   Lord William Campbell of Stracathro (attributed to). *Tullichewan Castle*, ca. 1857. Salted paper print; image: 21.3 x 28.6 cm., mount: 35.6 x 46.7 cm.

CATALOGUE NO. H4. Charles Marville. *Vue du Pont de la Réforme, ou Pont Louis-Philippe,* Paris, 18 February 1853. Salted paper print from a paper negative; image: 25.4 x 35 cm., mount: 44.2 x 61.9 cm.

H4

Charles Marville, 1816–1879

Vue du Pont de la Réforme, ou Pont Louis-Philippe, **Paris, 18 February 1853**

Salted paper print from a paper negative, printed by the firm of Louis-Désiré Blanquart-Evrard of Lille; signed and dated in the negative; image: 25.4 x 35 cm., mount: 44.2 x 61.9 cm.
Plate 29 of an album of 33 entitled *Paris photographique*, issued by Blanquart-Evrard from 1851 to 1853 (Jammes, 1981, p. 259)

Charles Marville is best remembered today for his many photographs of the streets of medieval Paris taken from the mid-1860s, prior to their demolition by Baron George Haussmann under Napoléon III's urban renewal plan. This view of the Pont de la Réforme, however, was taken more than a decade earlier, when Marville had only recently established himself as a full-time photographer.

Marville began his career as a painter-engraver. His early illustrative work is well represented at the Houghton Library, including his vignettes for Charles Nodier's *La Seine et ses bords* (1836), and his charming designs for the Curmer, 1838 edition of Bernardin de Saint-Pierre's *Paul et Virginie.* In 1851, at age thirty-five, Marville switched to photography, the very same year that Louis-Désiré Blanquart-Evrard established his photographic and publishing business in Lille. Blanquart-Evrard's firm printed the work of independent photographers, such as the salted paper prints from Maxime Du Camp's paper negatives for his *Egypte, Nubie, Palestine et Syrie* of 1852 (see above no. 18). The firm did its own publishing as well, working with such photographers as Thomas Sutton, Louis-Rémy Robert, John Stewart, and Henri Le Secq, and releasing a number of ambitious archaeological, architectural, and topographical albums during the four years of its existence.

Marville stands as the closest and most prolific of the professional photographers associated with Blanquart-Evrard. More than a hundred of his photographs are recorded among the albums published by the firm (Jammes, 1981, pp. 56–59, 171). Such is the case with the Vue du Pont de la Réforme. It belongs to *Paris photographique*, an album of thirty-three plates, mostly anonymous, to which Marville and Henri Le Secq contributed. The album was issued from 1851 to 1853, in fascicles of three to six plates each. The *Vue du Pont,* captured on a damp, snowy day, exemplifies Marville's careful composition and atmospheric rendering of Paris, for which he is famous. Only two copies of this rare and early print are recorded, one in André Jammes' collection, the other in the Horblit collection (Janis, "Seeing, Having, Knowing," 1989, p. 17, note 27).

H5
French School

Close-up of Chimeras on the South Tower of Notre-Dame de Paris, ca. 1870

Albumen silver print; image: 28 x 38 cm., mount: 29.6 x 39.6 cm.

In 1831, at age twenty-nine, Victor Hugo fired the imagination of his contemporaries with a novel in which he cast the medieval structure of Notre-Dame de Paris as its main character. Ravaged by centuries of neglect and the destruction caused by the French Revolution, the building was in great need of repair and Hugo's book catalyzed public opinion. Romantic champions of the Middle Ages, Catholics and monarchists in search of their grand tradition and glorious past, architectural historians, and conservationists all joined in supporting the renovation of Notre-Dame. The building was cited for renovation in 1841, and by 1843, Eugène Viollet-Le-Duc and Jean-Baptiste-Antoine Lassus presented their massive plan. It involved, besides structural work, the restoration of the entire sculptural program of Notre-Dame, including the hundreds of statues defaced by the Revolution, and the fantastic beings and gargoyles of the upper part of the cathedral.

The design of these monstrous beings possibly best reveals Viollet-Le-Duc's creative genius, his ability to connect with the fantastic imagination of the Middle Ages. His drawings for the recreation of the chimeras were done in 1848–1849, and the creatures were in place by 1850. These mid-nineteenth century recreations have come to stand for Notre-Dame itself and for what we think of as the spirit of the Middle Ages. Photography played an important role in this transference. It offered to the eye and the imagination creatures perched too high to be seen from the ground. Photography also provided models for the thousands of engraved and lithographed illustrations made to satisfy the craving of the time for all things medieval. As early as 1853, architectural photographer and medievalist Henri Le Secq captured the chimeras overlooking the city from the South Tower. The same year, Charles Nègre took an evocative portrait of Le Secq amid the creatures of the North Tower. He stood behind the beak-headed, melancholy vampire immortalized by Charles Meryon in his 1853 etching, "Le Stryge" (Janis, 1976).

As the moss and patina on the beasts' shoulders reveal, this anonymous close-up of chimeras was taken years later. Today just as then, the viewer is thrilled by the view of the fantastic, malevolent, terrifying beings lusting after the city and its inhabitants.

H6

Albert Sands Southworth, 1811–1894, and Josiah Johnson Hawes, 1808–1901 (attributed to)

View of Boston from the State House, Looking Southwest, 1857 or 1858

Plate [six] of a ten-plate panorama of Boston
Salted paper print; image: 45.7 x 58.7 cm., mount: 46 x 58.7 cm.

Both Southworth and Hawes saw daguerreotypes for the first time at one of the lectures given by François Gouraud, Daguerre's agent, who toured the East Coast in 1839 and 1840. Soon afterward, Southworth mastered the process sufficiently to open a photography studio in Boston, first with Joseph Pennell, then with Josiah Johnson Hawes. The alliance with Hawes was strengthened in 1849 when Hawes married Southworth's sister Nancy, a colorist at the studio. For eighteen years the Southworth and Hawes studio at 5 Tremont Row (later renumbered 19) offered its patrons the finest-quality photography. As the partners advertised in an undated broadside (now in the collection of the Museum of Fine Arts, Boston), "In style of execution and picturesque effect—in boldness of character and beauty of expression—in variety of size, and delicacy of lights and shadows—we shall aim at the highest perfection possible."

Best known for their daguerreotypes, Southworth and Hawes also excelled in making photographs on paper. This print, attributed to the studio, is one of ten views that together form a 360° panorama of Boston taken from the top of the State House. This view is number six in the series, looking southwest over the Boston Common and down Tremont Street. The Common, purchased in 1634, is the oldest urban park in the United States, and many newly planted trees can be seen in this photograph. At the far left of the photograph, at the corner of Tremont and Temple Place, is the old Masonic Temple with its twin towers. Boylston Street crosses Tremont at the right side of the photograph, along the lower end of the Boston Common. The first large building on Boylston, at the corner of Tremont, is the Hotel Pelham and across the street is John Quincy Adams's house. The second large building from the corner is the original Boston Public Library which opened to the public on New Year's Day, 1858. While the ladies entered the library directly for the opening ceremonies that day, gentlemen were asked to congregate at City Hall. They proceeded to march, with bands and military guard, up School Street to the State House, down Tremont to Boylston, and finally, into the new library building. Just behind the corner of Boylston and Tremont is St. James Church and in the distance, ships can be seen docked in South Cove. A complete set is held by the Boston Public Library and several prints each are at the Boston Athenaeum and the Bostonian Society. Some of the glass plate negatives still survive in private hands (see also R40 below).

CATALOGUE NO. H6.   Albert Sands Southworth and Josiah Johnson Hawes (attributed to). *View of Boston from the State House Looking Southwest*, 1857 or 1858. Salted paper print, image: 45.7 x 58.7 cm., mount: 46 x 58.7 cm.

C A T A L O G U E   N O.   H7.   Gustave Le Gray. *Brig upon the Water,* ca. 1856. Albumen silver print from a wet collodion on glass negative; image: 31.5 x 41 cm., mount: 53.5 x 66.3 cm.

H7
Gustave Le Gray, 1820–1882

Brig upon the Water, **Normandy, ca. 1856**

Albumen print from a wet collodion on glass negative; signature stamped in red on the print;
Le Gray's blind stamp on the mount; image: 31.5 x 41 cm., mount: 53.5 x 66.3 cm.
From the collection of Sir Thomas Phillipps

Gustave Le Gray is known as the major protagonist of paper negative photography in France. A painter used to experimenting with his own pigments, Le Gray approached photography as a technical innovator, a theorist, and a teacher. He modified Talbot's calotype process, introducing his own dry waxed-paper process (papier ciré sec) in the *Traité pratique de photographie sur papier et sur verre,* which he published in Paris in June 1850. The waxed-paper process was for Le Gray as much a means of artistic expression as it was a technique. He favored the soft tones and the textural gradations that he could achieve with paper negatives. Nevertheless, he experimented as well with collodion on glass.

The years 1856 to 1859 marked a transition in Le Gray's work. He turned from architectural and portraiture subjects to seascapes—the beaches and skies of the Normandy and Mediterranean coasts—favoring collodion on glass negatives and albumen prints for this series. He exhibited the seascapes at the Photographic Society in London, where they won immediate critical acclaim. It is probably on this occasion that Sir Thomas Phillipps acquired three of them including this one (Janis, *Invention,* exhibition brochure, 1989, no. 18).

Brig upon the Water stands as the most remarkable of the lot, as it captures all at once the light emerging through the clouds and the bright reflection on the water. Le Gray is known for having used a combination method for some of his seascapes, combining two negatives, one for the sea and one for the sky, to obtain richer results. This is not the case here. The Brig is captured in, and printed from, a single negative. Le Gray's experimental, unorthodox approach to printing technique is evident in the warm color, texture, and depth he has achieved in the *Brig.* Known for the sharpness of its effects as compared with the paper negative, the collodion negative was transformed by Le Gray to render soft contours and delicate gradations of tone. Le Gray advocated deemphasizing some of the details in order to obtain a more intense, overall effect (Janis, 1987, p. 204), which is precisely what he achieves here. The silhouette of the brig and the faint and blurry figures of the horses by the water contribute to the mystery of the scene, accentuating rather than taking away from the unique interplay of light through clouds and reflections on the water.

H8

James Anderson, 1813–1877

Bas-relief, South Side of the Arch of Titus, Rome, ca. 1860

Albumen silver print; image: 37.1 x 28.3 cm., mount: 64.5 x 49.2 cm.
Blind stamped on the mount "Libreria Tedesca/di/Giuse Spithöver/in Roma"

Born Isaac Atkinson, British artist James Anderson studied painting in Paris before settling in Rome around 1838. By the late 1840s Anderson had learned to make photographs, and in 1853, he opened a studio of his own, competing with such masters as Robert Macpherson. Anderson gradually became one of the leading commercial photographers in Rome, specializing in reproductions of works of art. He formed an arrangement with the well-established publisher and print dealer, Giuseppe Spithöver, whose blind stamp can be found on Anderson's mounts, distinguishing them from almost identical views by Macpherson. Anderson's son, Domenico, learned photography and a family-run business thrived well into the twentieth century. The Horblit collection contains 124 photographs by or attributed to Anderson.

The Arch of Titus stands along the path of the Via Sacra, leading to the south end of the Roman Forum. Commemorating the victory of Emperors Vespasian and Titus over the Jews, the arch was erected some time after Titus's death in 81 A.D. It was partially dismantled in the Middle Ages but was restored by Giuseppe Valadier in 1821; much of the sculpted relief we

CATALOGUE NO. H8.   James Anderson. *Bas-relief, South Side of the Arch of Titus*, ca. 1860. Albumen silver print; image: 37.1 x 28.3 cm., mount: 64.5 x 49.2 cm.

CATALOGUE NO. H9.   Harriet C. Tytler and Robert Christopher Tytler. *Unidentified Indian Tomb,*
1858? Albumenized salted paper print; image: approximately 48.3 x 38.4 cm.

see today dates from that work. However the central relief, depicted in this photograph, remains intact.

"On the inner compartment of the Arch of Titus is sculptured, in deep relief, the desolation of a city," wrote Percy Shelley. "The rapine and licence of a barbarous and enraged soldiery are imaged in the distance. The foreground is occupied by a procession of the victors, bearing in their profane hands . . . the sacred instruments of the eternal worship of the Jews" (Hare, p. 156). Shelley's account was not an exaggeration. Titus was appointed by Nero to suppress the uprising in Judea. He succeeded by building a wall around the city and waiting for the Jews to starve. In a three-day celebration of their victory, Titus's soldiers raped and slaughtered most of their prisoners, ransacking the temple of Herod of its sacred trumpets, the seven-branched candelabrum, the menorah, and other instruments of worship. As depicted in the arch relief, Titus rode back to Rome carrying with him the most valuable treasures of the Jews. According to the Talmud, the spoils of the temple were then flung into the Tiber where they remain today. No fewer than thirty-two prints and negatives in the Horblit collection are views of this very dramatic monument, taken by at least seven different photographers.

H9
Harriet C. Tytler, 1828–1907, and Robert Christopher Tytler, 1818–1872
Unidentified Indian Tomb, Delhi?, 1858?

Albumenized salted paper print; image: approximately 48.3 x 38.4 cm.
Written in pencil in a contemporary hand on the verso of the mount: "Gooeary Temple"

The daughter of a British military officer, Harriet Tytler was born in Oudh, a former province of British India. Although she was sent back to England during her childhood, she returned at age eighteen to spend the rest of her life in India. An independent woman with remarkable self-confidence, Harriet married Captain Robert Tytler in 1848 but lived and traveled alone a great deal. She was devoted to her husband and remained with him throughout the mutiny of Delhi in May 1857, even though she was eight months pregnant. Robert was a captain in the thirty-eighth Native Infantry. When his entire regiment rebelled against their British officers, Robert sought out the European civilians hiding in a small tower and led them safely out of the city. In the heat of that Indian summer Harriet gave birth to her third child in a small, straw-covered cart on a ridge overlooking Delhi.

Harriet Tytler was not a trained artist but received lessons in drawing as a child and often practiced by copying paintings owned by friends. When Captain Tytler received a two-year leave from the service in 1852, they traveled to Glasgow, London, and Paris and saw "all we could, even the exhibitions" (Tytler, p. 92). If they had not been introduced to photography earlier, they certainly were during this trip. After the 1857 mutiny, when Delhi was retaken and the Tytlers returned, orders were given for the troops to destroy a large area of native houses. Harriet found supplies and a six-by-eighteen-foot canvas, and painted a panoramic view of the city to preserve the scene. At some point in the next few years, she also began to make photographs.

Although her memoirs never mention when she learned photography, she and her husband made at least 300 calotypes, many as large as 15 x 20". In 1858, the family took a six-month vacation in Mussoorie before settling in Calcutta. We can assume that much of this time was spent making photographs, as the prints were exhibited by the Photographic Society of Bengal in 1859 and received great praise. The 27 views in the Horblit collection are primarily buildings at Lucknow, Agra, and the ruins of Delhi. The Tytlers again returned to London in the summer of 1860, bringing their work with them. Queen Victoria requested a viewing of Harriet's Delhi panorama, "along with the photographs taken two years later" (Tytler, p. 169) and many of the Tytlers's photographs were left at the India Office Library in London, where they can still be found. The Tytlers lived out their retirement in Simla, north of Delhi, Harriet founding an orphanage and Robert building a natural history museum.

H10
Pascal Sébah, 1838–1890

Marchandes ambulantes, Constantinople, ca. 1870

Albumen silver print, titled and signed in the negative; image: 21 x 27 cm.

Pascal Sébah, a Levantine, opened his photographic studio in Constantinople in 1857 at a time when photography was becoming popular in the city. Wichen, Kevork, and Hovsep Abdullah, known as the Abdullah Frères, opened their studio only a year later (see above no. 41). The Sultan himself took an interest in photography. At his orders, an Ottoman exhibition was prepared for the Vienna Universal Exhibition of 1873. It included artifacts from the treasury and a variety of costumes from all regions of the empire. For this occasion, the publication of a large album of photographs was undertaken. Sébah was commissioned to take 42 studio photographs of costumes, which he printed in the phototype method. These prints were accompanied by an introduction by Osman Hamdi Bey and Marie de Launay and were published in 1873 in an elaborate folio entitled, *Les costumes populaires de la Turquie.* Ernest Lacan, editor of *Le Moniteur de la Photographie*, commented in the September 15, 1873 issue of the journal, "We know that for a long time there have been very good photographers in Constantinople. We are sure of this because of the beautiful examples which have been sent to various exhibitions by Mr. Sébah and Mr. Abdullah, even including some of the latest methods being experimented on in France" (Çizgen, 1987, p. 79–80).

While his French assistant, A. Laroche, attended the studio, Sébah traveled widely, photographing the main attractions of Egypt, Nubia, Greece, Andrianople, and Smyrna. Archaeological finds, city views, local color, and portraits were offered in print or stereographic form to the active tourist trade. Sébah opened a branch in Cairo in 1884–1885 and took as his partner Policarpe Joaillier, another Frenchman already active in Constantinople; he changed the name of the firm to Sébah and Joaillier in 1888. This photography, taken on a Constantinople street, predates the association with Joaillier. Although it is one of several hundred such documentary scenes in Sebah's repertoire, it is striking in its naturalness and spontaneity. There are no special costumes here, no posed figures such as in *Les costumes populaires de la Turquie.* These are local women of the lower class engaged in selling the food that they have prepared. They have not even bothered to move for the camera. They look at it with an air of resignation and boredom, which says a lot about the prevalence of photographers and photography in Constantinople at the time.

CATALOGUE NO. H10. Pascal Sébah. *Marchandes ambulantes,* Constantinople, ca. 1870. Albumen silver print; image: 21 x 27 cm.

C ATALOGUE NO. H11.   Lewis Carroll (attributed to). *Portrait of a Seated Girl*, ca. 1860. Albumen silver print; image: 14.6 x 12.1 cm., mount: 38.1 x 27.3 cm.

H11

Lewis Carroll, 1832–1898 (attributed to)

Portrait of a Seated Girl, Oxford, ca. 1860

Albumen silver print; image: 14.6 x 12.1 cm., mount: 38.1 x 27.3 cm.

Reverend Charles Lutwidge Dodgson is best known by his pseudonym, Lewis Carroll. Educated at Christ Church, Oxford, Carroll accepted a position at the college as lecturer in mathematics and never left. He became a don in the surprisingly short time of five years, excelling in the study of logic. Although Carroll was introduced to photography by his uncle, it was not until he attended the 1856 annual exhibition of the Photographic Society that he was inspired to purchase equipment and begin making photographs. His earliest portraits were of the Oxford faculty and their families, particularly the daughters of Dean Liddell. Carroll enjoyed the company of children and filled his rooms at Christ Church with toys and games to please them. He often entertained the three Liddell sisters, telling them a particular story on July 4, 1862 that he would later publish as *Alice's Adventures in Wonderland.* Throughout that fall and winter the girls were Carroll's constant companions, often posing for photographs. This came to an abrupt end the following spring when Dodgson was banned from ever seeing them again. Although the relevant pages from his diary have been removed, it is assumed that he proposed marriage to the eleven-year-old Alice, an offer firmly rejected by her father.

By this time, Carroll had become a minor photographic celebrity, requested by Alfred Tennyson and the Rossettis. His camera gave him access to the homes of many famous artists and writers, including Ellen Terry, John Everett Millais, George MacDonald, and John Ruskin. The college allowed him to build a heated glass studio above his rooms where he could bring sitters year-round. He wrote several essays on photography and contracted with publisher Joseph Cundall to store and print his better work.

Still, his favorite subjects were always young girls. When Carroll found a potential model he would write to the child's mother requesting permission for her child to pose without clothing. "Their innocent unconsciousness is very beautiful, and gives one a feeling of reverence, as at the presence of something sacred," he wrote to one mother while assuring her, "I shall be quite prepared to find, next year, that they have learned to prefer dressed pictures. I am not so selfish as to wish for pictures, however valuable as works of art, the taking of which involved any risk for others" (Cohen, p. 171). In 1880, when gossip threatened his reputation at the college, Carroll gave up photographing nude children in his studio. Several years before his death he wrote directions for his funeral, including the note, "Please erase the following negatives: I would not like (for the families' sakes) the possibility of their getting into other hands. They are best erased by soaking in a solution of washing soda" (Dodgson, p. 4).

H12

Julia Margaret Cameron, 1815–1879

Charles Darwin, Freshwater, 1868

Albumen silver print; image: 29.5 x 24.4 cm., mount: 55.6 x 46.7 cm.
Colnaghi blind stamp on the mount, signed and dated by the photographer in ink on the recto of the mount, "Fresh Water from life registered photography (copy right) Julia Margaret Cameron Aug 1868/Ch. Darwin"

It is fitting that Cameron's first camera was a present from her family, in 1863, because photography soon dominated the family home in Freshwater on the Isle of Wight. Family members, Cameron's large circle of friends, and unsuspecting visitors were all cajoled into serving as her models. A glazed chickencoop was converted into her studio and a coal shed was transformed into her darkroom. Household servants were hired on the basis of their looks and had to leave their chores whenever Cameron needed them to pose, which often involved dressing up for elaborate tableaux vivants. Meals often waited until Cameron was satisfied with the day's glass plate negatives, and she admitted, "this habit of running into the dining-room with my wet pictures has stained an immense quantity of table linen . . . I should have been banished from any less indulgent household" (Cameron, p. 181).

However, Cameron was not content to remain an amateur photographer. She was an ambitious promoter of her photographs which she considered fine art. She hired three galleries for solo exhibitions, assembled presentation albums that she gave to influential friends and institutions, and actively pursued commercial sales of her photographs. In 1874, Cameron wrote an unfinished memoir, *Annals of My Glass House*, chronicling her obsession and her talent. When the century ended, she would have been pleased to know that she and Henry Talbot were the only nineteenth-century photographers included in the *British Dictionary of National Biography*.

On display is a portrait of the British scientist and founder of modern evolutionary theory, Charles Robert Darwin. Born in Shrewsbury, Shropshire, England, Darwin trained at the University of Cambridge and, in 1858 announced his controversial theory. *On the Origin of Species* was published the following year, and Darwin became an international celebrity. On July 16, 1868, Darwin and his family traveled to Freshwater for a summer holiday. Cameron invited the whole family to dinner and persuaded Darwin to sit for her. Quite taken with both Cameron and photography, Darwin wrote soon afterward to an old friend, botanist J. D. Hooker, "How about photographs? Can you spare time for a line to our dear Mrs. Cameron? She came to see us off, and loaded us with presents of photographs, and Erasmus called after her, 'Mrs. Cameron, there are six people in this house all in love with you.' When I paid her, she cried out, 'Oh what a lot of money!' and ran to boast to her husband" (F. Darwin, vol. 2, p. 283). Many copies of this portrait were sold with Darwin's inscription on the mount, "I like this photograph very much better than any other which has been taken of me." Four years later, he took great care in selecting photographic illustrations for his new book, *The Expression of the Emotions in Man and Animals* (see above no. 46).

CATALOGUE NO. H12.   Julia Margaret Cameron. *Charles Darwin*, 1868. Albumen silver print; image: 29.5 x 24.4 cm., mount: 55.6 x 46.7 cm.

H13
Roger Fenton, 1819–1869
General Cissé & Officers & Soldiers of Genl. Bosquet's Division, 1855

Salted paper print; image: 17.1 x 17.1 cm., mount: 58.4 x 42.9 cm.
Printed title and credit on full Agnew letterpress mount, "Deposé, Photographed by R. Fenton Manchester, Published by T. Agnew & Sons, March 25th, 1856/London, P. & D. Colnaghi & C. Paris, Moulin, 23, Rue Richer, New York, Williams & C."; written in red pencil on the verso of the mount, "137"

Roger Fenton has been called the greatest British photographer of the nineteenth century, an impressive title for someone who practiced photography for only a little over ten years. A solicitor by profession, Fenton also studied painting and learned photography sometime around 1850. By 1852 he was already a major force, proposing the organization of a British photographic society and, along with Joseph Cundall and Philip Delamotte, organizing the first exhibition devoted to the art. He was named the Photographic Society's first honorary secretary and, in 1854, was chosen over Philip Delamotte as the first official photographer for the British Museum.

Fenton is best known for his photographs of the Crimean War. With 2 assistants, 3 horses, 5 cameras, 700 glass plates, 36 large chests, and a converted wine-merchant's van for a darkroom, Fenton landed in the Balaklava harbor on March 8, 1855. The trip was financed by the Manchester publishing firm of Thomas Agnew & Sons but was also sanctioned by the government. Prince Albert provided letters of introduction. During his first two months Fenton described the light and temperature as "everything that a photographer could desire," and he was able to make almost instantaneous pictures. "Towards the end of April, 3 seconds were frequently enough for the proper exposure" (Fenton, p. 288). However, as the summer approached, the heat became unbearable, and he was forced to stop work each morning by nine or ten o'clock.

Fenton relied on the hospitality of the officers he met along the way, "now living in luxury and abundance, and now in want; occasionally sleeping in a general's marquee, and sometimes on the bare ground" (Fenton, p. 290). Much of his correspondence describes the dinners, champagne, and cigars he shared with these men. His talents were in constant demand, but rarely to capture scenes of battle. "Everybody is bothering me for their portrait to send home," complained Fenton (Gernsheim, 1954, p. 58). Of the 59 Crimean photographs in the Horblit collection, 40 are portraits of the officers. The photograph on display was probably taken around May 6, 1855, when Fenton wrote to his wife, "I moved my van to General Bosquet's quarters . . . . I made a group with General Cissé the Chief of the Staff in the centre . . . . After breakfast the officers got together a quantity of soldiers of different corps, Zouaves, chasseurs, &c. I made several fine pictures of them" (Gernsheim, 1954, pp. 73–74).

Fenton lasted until the failed siege of Sebastopol on June 18. "I felt quite unequal to further exertion," Fenton later told the Photographic Society. He left for home infected with cholera. In September, 312 of his negatives were printed and exhibited in London, then published by subscription between November 1855 and April 1856. However, with a peace treaty signed in March, the British public soon lost interest in the war. Many prints were left unsold and auctioned, along with similar views by James Robertson, at the end of the year. Fenton went back to work for the British Museum and in 1862 gave up photography completely, for reasons unknown.

CATALOGUE NO. H13.   Roger Fenton. *General Cissé & Officers & Soldiers of Genl. Bosquet's Division*, 1855. Salted paper print; image: 17.1 x 17.1 cm., mount: 58.4 x 42.9 cm.

H14

Félix Teynard, 1817–1892

Karnak (Thèbes) Sphinx à tête humaine et à tête de bélier, en Y, 1851–1852

Salted paper print from a waxed-paper negative, printed by H. de Fonteny et Cie.; image: 24 x 30.4 cm., mount: 40.1 x 51.8 cm.

Plate 68 of *Égypte et Nubie: Sites et monuments les plus intéressants pour l'étude de l'art et de l'histoire. Atlas photographié accompagné de plans et d'une table explicative servant de complément à la grande Description de l'Égypte.* Paris: Goupil et Cie, 1858.

From the collection of Sir Thomas Phillipps

Félix Teynard's early career as a civil engineer from Grenoble gave little indication of the adventurous spirit that would take him, in 1851, on a two-year trip to Egypt and Nubia. Little is known of his photographic training, but he returned with more than 160 publishable waxed-paper negatives for his *Égypte et Nubie: Sites et monuments les plus intéressants pour l'étude de l'art et de l'histoire.* These were printed in Paris by H. De Fonteny et Cie, a commercial firm established in 1851, a few months after that of Blanquart-Evrard in Lille.

One must admire the audacity of this thirty-four-year-old, who intended his work to complement photographically the *Description de l'Égypte.* The *Description* was the opus commissioned by the French government as the official record of the scientific and archaeological discoveries made during Napoléon I's Egyptian campaign of 1798–99. Published in Paris from 1809 to 1822, this monumental work includes no less than 11 volumes of text, more than 900 plates, and an atlas so large that a special piece of furniture was designed to hold it. Teynard was ready to concede that, in some areas, the camera could not compete with the hands of the draftsmen accompanying the earlier expedition. In particular, "the total darkness in the tombs and in the temples . . . does not allow one to photograph the most harmonious and remarkable paintings that decorate the walls" (Introduction, p. 1). Yet, as this print makes evident, Teynard felt sure that the camera far surpassed the careful work of the best of draftsmen in capturing at a bold angle the physical mass of a monument, the vastness and desolation of the landscape, the sharp contrast of light and shadow, the grainy texture of stone and the ubiquitous presence of sand.

This print was one of twenty-two of Teynard's photographs of Egypt in Sir Thomas Phillipps's collection, which Horblit acquired en bloc in 1961. Horblit complemented them with photographs of Egypt and Nubia by Maxime Du Camp, Francis Frith, and Richard Morris Hunt, among others (see above case 4). Additional holdings at the Houghton Library include two original drawings by Antoine Cécile for the *Description de l'Égypte*, a magnificent copy of the *Description* itself, and both the London and New York 1803 editions of Vivant Denon's *Voyage dans la Basse et Haute Égypte pendant les campagnes du Général Bonaparte.*

CATALOGUE NO. H14. Félix Teynard. *Karnak (Thèbes) Sphinx à tête humaine et à tête de bélier, en Y*, 1851–52. Salted paper print from a waxed paper negative; image: 24 x 30.4 cm., mount: 40.1 x 51.8 cm.

H15
Félix Bonfils, 1831–1885

Colonne Pompée et cimetière, Alexandria, before 1876
Albumen silver print; image: 21 x 27.5 cm.

Seduced by the beauties of Lebanon, which he visited as a member of a French military expedition in 1860, Félix Bonfils returned to Beirut in 1867 with his wife and son, Adrien. There he established a photographic studio, soon branching out to Cairo, Alexandria, and Alès, France. The young Adrien was sent to France to finish his schooling. Upon his return to Lebanon in 1878, at the age of seventeen, Adrien took charge of the photography while his parents continued to manage the studio.

During the early years of the business, before Adrien joined him, Félix traveled to Egypt and Palestine, Syria, Greece, and Constantinople, taking more than 1,600 views of architectural, archaeological, biblical, and ethnographic interest (R. Thomas, p. 34). He published *Souvenirs d'Orient* in 1878, a five-volume album of photographic plates with descriptive captions documenting the most important sites, cities, and ruins he had visited. This photograph of Pompey's column and the Muslim cemetery in Alexandria was probably taken before 1876. A *Colonne Pompée* is listed as one of 677 views for sale in the first Bonfils catalogue—*Catalogue des vues photographiques de l'Orient*—published in Alès in 1876. Each photograph could be purchased as a print in three different sizes, or as a stereoscopic view.

Félix Bonfils died in France in 1885. Adrien maintained his father's high standards until 1894, when he sold Photographie Bonfils to Abraham Guiragossian, a photographer from Palestine established in Beirut. During the same period, Professor David Gordon Lyon, appointed first curator of the Semitic Museum at Harvard University, started a collection of photographs that would soon number close to 1,750. Among them were photographs by Antonio Beato and the Fratelli Alinari, as well as some 500, pre-1890 photographs from the Bonfils studio. These were inventoried by Carney E. S. Gavin in *The Image of the East: Photographs by Bonfils from the Harvard Semitic Museum* (1982). Today, the photographs are part of the Visual Collections of the Fine Arts Library at Harvard University, where the entire Semitic Museum collection of near 37,500 photographs was transferred in 1995. These Bonfils holdings, together with those in the Fogg Art Museum and the Horblit collection, constitute an extensive archive of early Near Eastern photography.

CATALOGUE NO. H15.   Félix Bonfils. *Colonne Pompée et cimetière*, Alexandria, before 1876. Albumen silver print; image: 21 x 27.5 cm.

H16
Alphonse J. Liébert, 1827–1914
St. Cloud Incendié. Place d'Armes, côté de l'Eglise, Paris, ca. 1871

Albumen silver print; image: 18.1 x 25.1 cm., mount: 32.8 x 41.5 cm.
Caption letterpress-printed on the mount
Plate 56 from a two-volume set, *Les ruines de Paris et de ses environs, 1870–1871.* Cent photographies par A. Liébert, texte par Alfred d'Aunay. Paris: Editées par La Photographie Américaine Alphonse Liébert, 1871.

Without the photographs of the period, it would be hard to conceive of the destruction inflicted on Paris by the Franco-Prussian war and the Commune insurrection in 1870–1871. Only a decade after the grand urban renewal project undertaken by Baron George Haussmann (see above H4) and the renovation efforts of Eugène Viollet-Le-Duc and Antoine Lassus (H5), Paris was reduced to ruins. Alphonse Liébert's two-volume photographic album, *Les ruines de Paris et de ses environs, 1870–1871,* accompanied by Alfred d'Aunay's descriptive account, offered then as it does now, the fullest visual account of Paris's martyrdom.

The first album documents the destruction caused by the Commune (March–May 1871) and the ruins of some of the most important buildings in the city, including the Tuileries, Hôtel de Ville, Palais Royal, and the Colonne Vendôme, felled by revolutionary fury. The second album is devoted to what remained of the towns surrounding Paris after they were bombarded and systematically burned by the Prussians. One such town was Saint Cloud, a popular place for a rendez-vous during the Second Empire. Little remained of the small town and the lovely houses above the bank of the river, site of leisurely Sunday strolls. Gone was its famous restaurant, La Tête Noire, which Liébert had photographed in happier times. This print of the Place d'Armes is part of a group of eleven photographs removed from the original albums. Horblit also acquired a complete set of albums. The typeface used for the letterpress captions of the eleven individual prints differs from that of the other edition, dating possibly from 1872.

Throughout his career, Liébert boasted the logo, "Photographie Américaine." It referred to his experience as a photographer in America, first in San Francisco, where he settled at age twenty-four in 1851, then in Nevada City, California, where he operated a Daguerreian studio from 1857 to 1862. The catchy logo was also intended to appeal to a public that associated America with technological progress (McCauley, p. 65–66). Liébert himself was an innovator, known for his invention of a solar enlarger and, much later in his career, for opening and perfecting the first studio equipped with electric light for the purpose of making exposures (Palmquist, p. 160). A successful author, Liébert's works included a manual entitled, not surprisingly, *La Photographie en Amérique, traité pratique contenant les découvertes les plus récentes.* It received as many as four editions between 1864 and 1884. The Horblit collection contains the third (1878) edition.

CATALOGUE NO. H16.   Alphonse J. Liébert. *St. Cloud Incendié. Place d'Armes, côté de l'Eglise*, ca. 1871.
Albumen silver print; image: 18.1 x 25.1 cm., mount: 32.8 x 41.5 cm.

CASE 1

Women and Children

CATALOGUE NO. R1.   W. T. Schneider. *Stereoscopic Portrait of a Seated Woman*. Quarter plate daguerreotypes

R1
W. T. Schneider, 1839–1921
Stereoscopic Portrait of a Seated Woman

Quarter plate daguerreotypes

Stamped on the gilt mat of this daguerreotype is the name "W. T. Schneider." This almost certainly refers to Wilhelm Schneider, son of Trudepert Schneider, a German photographer who specialized in stereoscopic daguerreotypes. Trudepert (or Trutpert) was a carpenter living in Ehrenstetten when he met the Parisian daguerreotypist J. Broglie. Schneider apprenticed with Broglie, traveling throughout Germany and Switzerland. His sons, William and Heinrich, joined their father and in 1858, established the studio of T. Schneider & Soehne based in Cologne (Kempe, p. 243). Working in Germany and northern Italy, they offered architectural and portrait photographs but were best known for their stereoscopic views. The two sons worked briefly in Hamburg and then in Berlin, traveling as far as Moscow in 1861 to photograph heads of state. They continued the family business until Heinrich's death in 1900.

As a result of the tremendous popularity of stereoscopic viewers at the Great Exhibition of 1851, a number of photographers began experimenting with stereoscopic images of all kinds. John F. Mascher, in Philadelphia, and Antoine Claudet, in London, patented similar stereoscopic daguerreotype cases in March 1853. The cases include two almost identical daguerreotypes and two lenses on a hinged flap. Unfortunately, daguerreotypes are difficult to see in the best circumstances, and these attached spectacles rarely brought the scene into focus. In 1854, Frederick Langenheim began to manufacture stereoscopic views on glass and paper and founded the American Stereoscopic Company. The London Stereoscopic Company, Henry T. Anthony & Company, and Negretti and Zambra were only a few of the other firms that successfully marketed stereoscopic views, which remained popular well into the twentieth century.

Catalogue no. R2.   John McElroy. *Portrait of a Boy Seated on a Sofa with a Dog.* Sixth plate daguerreotype

R2
John McElroy
Portrait of a Boy Seated on a Sofa with a Dog
Sixth plate daguerreotype

The Horblit collection includes eleven excellent daguerreotypes by John McElroy (see also R19 below) about whom little is known. An 1859 directory lists a daguerreotypist by that name working in Locke, New York. An entry in *Craig's Daguerreian Registry* suggests that the same McElroy may have also operated in Auburn, New York, although the dates are unknown. It is not unusual to see fine examples of daguerreotypes from small-town operators, such as McElroy. At the cost of approximately two dollars, daguerreotypes were available in most areas either from small studios or traveling photographers. To understand the number of commercial photographers practicing outside big cities, it is helpful to look at government census figures. In the census of 1850, for instance, New York State listed a total of 600 professional artists, 240 of whom were practicing daguerreotypists *(Daguerreian Annual* 1993, p. 116). That same year, *Humphrey's Journal* documented 77 daguerreotype studios in New York City staffed by 127 operators. Simple arithmetic shows 113 photographers were practicing outside New York City in the small towns spread throughout the state (Newhall, 1976, p. 55).

Few of these photographers became famous. The Horblit collection contains many daguerreotypists by photographers who, like McElroy, never became well known, such as (from New York State) A. J. Beals, M. S. Hagaman, J. C. Helme, Silas A. Holmes, Nathaniel Jaquith, T. S. Jube, Samuel N. Rice, Josiah Thompson, Thomas S. Walsh, Peter Welling, and Robert Weston. Their bread-and-butter portraits constitute the strongest part of the Horblit collection, which documents the phenomenal growth and development of this art form both within and outside the major, commmercial markets.

R3
Jeremiah Gurney, 1812–1895
Portrait of Two Standing Girls

Half plate daguerreotype

One of the first and most enterprising photographers in America was Jeremiah Gurney (see also R29). Gurney was operating a jewelry store in New York City when he learned to make daguerreotypes sometime around 1840. Like many of his contemporaries, Gurney opened a daguerreotype studio not long after his first lesson. He soon became a leading practitioner and was chosen in 1851 to exhibit at the Great Exhibition in London. Despite professional hardships, including a fire in his gallery the following year, Gurney continued his business, purchasing and refurnishing Jesse Whitehurst's gallery at 349 Broadway. Known as the Palace of Art, the gallery is pictured and described in an advertisement in the Horblit collection: "This is the largest and most perfect Daguerreotype establishment in the United States, comprising nine spacious rooms, superbly furnished and devoted exclusively to the art. The RECEPTION SALOONS are adorned with the portraits of the most Distinguished Persons of the Age. The operating department is under the personal supervision of the proprietor, and contains three immense skylights, arranged on scientific principles, for the admission of one unbroken and steady flood of light, the thing most essential to secure a favorable picture."

During his thirty-four years in business, Gurney was linked with many other successful photographers and inventors. In 1852 he formed a brief partnership with A. Litch, in 1853 employed Solomon N. Carvalho, and in 1855 formed a partnership with another former apprentice, Charles DeForest Fredricks (see below R42). In 1857, Gurney joined John Bishop Hall, who had a patent on the hallotype. The process brought together two albumen photographs—one translucent with wax, the other hand-colored—in the attempt to produce a three-dimensional image. For about a year, hallotypes caused great excitement in the photographic literature. The February 15 cover of *Humphrey's Journal* announced, "Hall & Gurney have received some three thousand applications for Rights to practice their Process." Although the rights and equipment sold for less than eight dollars, the claim of "astonishing stereoscopic relief . . . surpassing that of the most brilliant daguerreotype . . . in sublime harmony" was greatly exaggerated, and Gurney quickly moved on. His son, Benjamin, was with the firm from 1860 until 1874, when the gallery finally closed. The Horblit collection includes 19 daguerreotypes by or attributed to Jeremiah Gurney, and the Houghton Library owns one of Gurney's few surviving 1857 hallotypes.

R4

American School

Portrait of Three Women, One Man, Two Boys, and a Girl

Whole plate daguerreotype

R5

American School

Portrait of a Seated Woman Holding Flowers

Whole plate daguerreotype in oval frame

R6

American School

Portrait of a Girl Seated on a Table Beside a Wooden Sled

Sixth plate daguerreotype

R7

J. Baum

Portrait of Two Women in Front of a Painted Backdrop, ca. 1850

Quarter plate daguerreotype

R8

American School

Portrait of a Man, a Baby, and Two Women, One in a Servant's Outfit

Quarter plate daguerreotype

Catalogue no. R11. French School. *Portrait of a Woman Seated in an Ornate Chair.* Mammoth plate daguerreotype

R9

American School

Portrait of a Standing Woman in Back of Three Boys and a Girl, All Dressed Identically

Half plate daguerreotype

R10

American School

Portrait of Three Women and One Man

Whole plate daguerreotype

R11

French School

Portrait of a Woman Seated in an Ornate Chair

Mammoth plate daguerreotype

R12

American School

Portrait of a Girl Standing on a Chair Beside a Table

Quarter plate daguerreotype with gem tintype of girl attached to cover glass

R13

Adolphe Legros

Portrait of a Standing Girl

Quarter plate daguerreotype

CASE 2

Outdoors, Architecture, and Animals

CATALOGUE NO. R14. American School. *View of the Steinway Building, New York City,* 1875 or later. Half plate daguerreotype

R14
American School
View of the Steinway Building, New York City, **1875 or later**

Half plate daguerreotype

This daguerreotype shows a rare outdoor view of New York City, possibly taken from the roof of Columbia College at 50th Street on the west side of Park Avenue, looking north. Like most daguerreotypes, the scene is laterally reversed. It focuses on the Steinway Building, with the 59th Street Bridge and the Greek Orthodox churches of Astoria, Queens, visible in the background. The site of the Steinway Building, at 375 Park Avenue, is now occupied by the Seagram's Building.

Heinrich Engelhard Steinweg and his family moved to New York City in 1850 and found great success building pianos. When they needed to expand their factory, the Steinwegs decided on an area now bordered by Park and Lexington Avenues, between 52nd and 53rd Streets. The price of the land was low because of the noisy steam engines of the New York & Harlem Railroad, which ran along Park (or Fourth) Avenue. The factory opened to much acclaim in August of 1860 and became known as the Steinway Building some time after 1864, when Heinrich Steinweg changed his name to Henry Steinway.

Exasperated with the congestion and pollution the railroad caused, local residents forced its owner, Cornelius Vanderbilt, to agree to place the tracks below ground. Work began at Grand Central Station in 1873. Two years later, the open track had been covered from 51st Street to 97th Street, with a fifteen-foot sidewalk added on either side, as seen in this daguerreotype. The fact that this daguerreotype was made well after the heyday of American daguerreotyping adds to the appeal of an already exceptional image.

R15
American School
Portrait of Mr. and Mrs. Henry R. Campbell with Horse and Wagon, 1847
Quarter plate daguerreotype; plate maker, Scovill Manufacturing Company

This is a view of Henry R. Campbell's home, in Lebanon, New Hampshire, located on the corner of two streets that are now known as Bank and Campbell Streets. Henry Campbell was a prominent inventor and engineer in New England and in Washington, D.C. For his hometown, Campbell designed and constructed the West Lebanon bridge across the Connecticut River. The bridge provided area merchants with an important link to White River Junction, where the new Central Vermont Railroad provided a direct route to Boston. The bridge was to be completed the year this daguerreotype was made but in fact did not open until June 1848. Although the date of Campbell's death is not known, his home was purchased in 1859 by Henry Carter, the merchant prince of northern New England, and the Carter House, as it came to be known, has been preserved as a historic landmark. Both this portrait and a half plate daguerreotype of Campbell alone (see R38) were part of the Josephine Cobb collection of daguerreotypes (R28).

R16
Platt D. Babbitt, died 1879
View of Niagara Falls, ca. 1855
Half plate daguerreotype

CATALOGUE NO. R17. Platt D. Babbitt. *View of Tourists at Prospect Point, Niagara Falls*, ca. 1855. Whole plate daguerreotype

R17
Platt D. Babbitt, died 1879
View of Tourists at Prospect Point, Niagara Falls, ca. 1855

Whole plate daguerreotype

Platt Babbitt was not the first photographer to capture Niagara Falls, but as early as 1852, he held a franchise for commercial photography on the American side of the falls. Already a popular tourist attraction, the falls became cheaper and easier to travel to in 1853 with the completion of the Canandaigua and Niagara Falls Railroad. Also that year, the International Hotel, built by B.F. Childs, joined the Cataract House at Niagara Falls—two of the largest and best hotels in the country. Babbitt capitalized on the growth in the tourist trade, building a pavilion to shelter his equipment at a popular lookout point. He would photograph a group of tourists as they viewed the falls, develop the plate, and sell the daguerreotype to the sightseers before they departed. Thus, people often have their backs to the camera in Babbitt's photographs, as in this daguerreotype of nineteen tourists standing at the edge of Prospect Point.

This daguerreotype came to Horblit through the Josephine Cobb collection (see below R28). The Horblit collection has eight images of Niagara Falls by or attributed to Babbitt (three daguerreotypes and five glass stereoscopic views), as well as three unattributed ambrotypes of the falls.

R18

Dr. Samuel A. Bemis, 1793–1881

Self-portrait of Samuel Bemis with Buildings and the White Mountains in the Distance, ca. 1840
Whole plate daguerreotype

A Boston jeweler turned dentist, Samuel Bemis made his fortune as the inventor of usable false teeth. (Earlier, false teeth were primarily cosmetic and had to be removed before each meal.) Bemis learned photography from François Gouraud, a representative for Alphonse Giroux & Cie, which held the franchise for Daguerre's camera and equipment. Gouraud came to the United States in the fall of 1839 to promote the daguerreotype process through exhibitions and demonstrations. A receipt indicates that Bemis paid $76 for equipment and twelve daguerreotype plates in April 1840. Within a week of the purchase, he had made his first successful image.

Only about fifteen daguerreotypes by Bemis are known to exist today, half made in Boston and half in New Hampshire. Bemis spent his summers in the White Mountains of New Hampshire and built a home there, near Crawford Notch. He came to own a great deal of property in this area, including the well-known Unique Inn, near Hart's Location. After his death, Bemis Station was named for him. The figure visible at the bottom right in this daguerreotype is thought to be Bemis himself.

R19

John McElroy

View of Two Men in a Horse-Drawn Wagon
Sixth plate daguerreotype

R20

Photographer unknown

View of an Unidentified City Street
Whole plate daguerreotype

CATALOGUE NO. R24. Photographer unknown. *Exterior View of an Unidentified Two-Story Stucco Building*. Mammoth plate daguerreotype

R21

American School

Exterior View of a House

Quarter plate daguerreotype in frame

R22

American School

Portrait of a Man Seated in a Horse-Drawn Cart

Quarter plate daguerreotype

R23

Photographer unknown

View of an Unidentified City Street

Quarter plate daguerreotype

R24

Photographer unknown

Exterior View of an Unidentified Two-Story Stucco Building

Mammoth plate daguerreotype

R25

American School

Cat Drinking from a Bowl

Quarter plate daguerreotype

R26

Iller

View of Maisonnette pour Cerfs, Parc de San Donato, Florence, Italy, 1847

Whole plate daguerreotype

Case 3

Men and Their Work

R27
John Jabez Edwin Mayall, 1813–1901
Portrait of a Man, His Arm Resting on a Book, Seated in Front of a Painted Backdrop

Half plate daguerreotype

Born in Manchester, England, John Mayall (née Jabez Meal) moved to Philadelphia where he opened a daguerreotype studio in 1840. Around 1845, Mayall formed a partnership with Samuel Van Loan, another British expatriot practicing photography in Philadelphia. The partnership ended after only one year, when Mayall sold his studio to Marcus Root and returned to England. Claudet gave him a job at his gallery, but early in 1847, Mayall was advertising his own business, the American Daguerreotype Institution, under the name of Professor Highschool. The Horblit collection includes five hand-colored daguerreotypes made at Mayall's London studio during this period.

Mayall was at the height of his success during the Great Exhibition in 1851. There he exhibited 72 daguerreotypes, which caught Prince Albert's eye. The Queen and Prince Consort invited Mayall to Windsor to make a series of photographs of the royal family. His *Royal Album* was published in 1860. He also distributed *cartes de visite* from this series, which earned him a fortune (see above no. 23). Later, for the wedding of the Prince of Wales, Mayall built a complete glass-house studio at Windsor in which to create the wedding portfolio. The glass-house was then moved to Brighton, where Mayall spent his time from 1865 on, letting his sons take over more and more of the commercial business. Mayall continued to photograph, experimenting with a solar camera and making enlargements up to eight feet long. At his death in 1901, he was eulogized as the oldest photographer in England.

R28
American School
Portrait of a Seated Man in a Naval Uniform

Sixth plate daguerreotype, plate from Scovill Manufacturing Company

This occupational daguerreotype came to the Horblit collection as part of the Josephine Cobb collection. Horblit purchased her entire collection at a small auction, even though some of the exceptional views had been removed and sold separately. Cobb was a native of Portland, Maine, who studied American history and was trained in archive management. In 1936, she was the first woman hired as an archivist at the National Archives in Washington, D.C., and later became the head of the Still Pictures Division. During World War II, Cobb was accepted in a special government-sponsored course in basic photography and microfilming, which led to several promotions within the Archives. Her specialty became the history of Abraham Lincoln and the Civil War, and in 1958, she published the first substantial piece of research on Alexander Gardner's photography. She chose to collect daguerreotypes specifically to avoid any conflict with the collecting interests of the National Archives.

From 1960 until her retirement, Cobb worked as a specialist in iconography and came to national attention when she identified Abraham Lincoln's face in a photograph of a crowd at Gettysburg. When a new postage stamp was issued in 1984, commemorating the 50th anniversary of the National Archives, *Reader's Digest* marked the occasion by printing a cachet depicting Cobb at work with the famous Lincoln negative. She served on the board for the Civil War Centennial Commission, the Abraham Lincoln Sesquicentennial Commission, the Photographers' Hall of Fame for the American Museum of Photography, and the National Capital Landmarks Commission. Her life ended quietly back in Maine, in an oceanfront home she had designed with her lifetime companion, Pauline Pero. Josephine Cobb's collection of daguerreotypes and ambrotypes numbered 227, 132 of which have been identified so far in the Horblit collection (see also R15, R17, R34, and R38).

CATALOGUE NO. R29.   German School. *Portrait of an Eight-Man Bowling Team.* Half plate daguerreotype

R29

German School

Portrait of an Eight-Man Bowling Team

Half plate daguerreotype

R30

Jeremiah Gurney, 1812–1895

Portrait of a Man

Mammoth plate daguerreotype

R31

American School

Portrait of Two Seated Men, One Holding a Saw and One Holding a Hammer

Sixth plate daguerreotype

R32

American School

Portrait of a Standing Soldier Posed with a Sword

Quarter plate daguerreotype

R33

American School

Portrait of a Stonecutter

Sixth plate daguerreotype set into a marble base

R34

American School

Portrait of Jacob and Thomas Kesey

Sixth plate daguerreotype

R35

American School

Portrait of a Seated Man and a Dog

Sixth plate daguerreotype

CATALOGUE NO. R31. American School. *Portrait of Two Seated Men, One Holding a Saw and One Holding a Hammer*. Sixth plate daguerreotype

CATALOGUE NO. R34. American School. *Portrait of Jacob and Thomas Kesey*. Sixth plate daguerreotype

R36

American School

Portrait of a Man Holding a Hammer and a Candlestick

Sixth plate daguerreotype

R37

American School

Portrait of a Standing Man with His Hand Resting on a Fluted Column

Mammoth plate daguerreotype in wood frame

R38

American School

Portrait of Henry R. Campbell

Half plate daguerreotype

R39

American School

Portrait of a Seated Man

Whole plate daguerreotype in gesso frame

Case 4

Studio Portraits

R40

Josiah Johnson Hawes, 1808–1901

Portrait of Stephen Allen, 1847

Half plate daguerreotype

Two months after his eightieth birthday, Stephen Allen (1767–1852) traveled from his home in New York City to Tremont Row in Boston to have his portrait made at the studio of Southworth and Hawes, the finest portrait photographers of the period. Perhaps he was marking the end of a long and successful career, first as a merchant and philanthropist, then as a politician. Allen began work as an apprentice to a sail maker at the age of twelve, and ran a prosperous sail-making business of his own from 1791 to 1825. A zealous patriot, Allen was elected to New York City's common council in 1817 and quickly made his way to the head of Tammany Society. He was not only appointed mayor for three terms from 1821 to 1824, but was also elected grand sachem, or president, of the ruling Tammany council, a title he held for over ten years. He went on to serve as a New York State senator, water commissioner of New York City, and president of the National Democratic Party. Allen was an active member of many organizations, including the Mechanic and Scientific Institution of New-York, where he may have first encountered the new developments in photography. He died during the burning of the steamboat *Henry Clay*.

In 1847, the studio of Southworth and Hawes was at its height. The attribution of this portrait to Hawes was made by Horblit, who wrote it on the back of a torn blank check, as was his practice, and placed it behind the plate. A label pasted to the velvet cushion reads, "Original of/ Stephen Allen/1847/September." Hawes, a former painter, has always been considered the more artistic of the two photographers, while Southworth was more technically adept. They promoted this combination of talents in their advertisements: "One of the partners is a practical Artist, and as we never employ Operators, customers receive our personal attention" (*The Massachusetts Register* 1853, p. 326). Horblit must have felt that this portrait exhibited the aesthetic qualities of Hawes's work and therefore credited him alone. The Horblit collection contains nine daguerreotypes attributed to Southworth and Hawes, as well as two paper photographs: a panoramic view of Boston (see above H6) and the *Snow Scene on the Northeast Corner of the Boston Common*, made by Hawes alone around 1875. Hawes died at the age of ninety-four at Crawford Notch, New Hampshire, not far from the home of another early daguerreotypist, Samuel Bemis (see above R18).

R41

Mathew B. Brady, 1823?–1896

Portrait of a Man Seated between a Standing Girl and Boy

Half plate daguerreotype

The Horblit collection contains 13 daguerreotypes from the New York studios of Mathew Brady. Brady's imprint can be found on the velvet liner of the cases or stamped on the brass mats of the daguerreotypes. Whether Brady himself had anything to do with these photographs is doubtful. He acted as director of his daguerreotype galleries rather than as cameraman, a fact he did not attempt to hide, as noted in the April 1854 *Photographic and Fine Art Journal:* "Mr. B is not a practical operator, yet he displays superior management in his business and consequently deserves high praise for the lofty position he has attained in the daguerrean [sic] fraternity" (Panzer, p. xvii).

Brady became the best-known New York photographer of the nineteenth century, famous for both his daguerreotypes and his paper prints. He began his career in 1843, manufacturing the cases used to house daguerreotypes, and the following year opened his own Daguerrean [sic] Miniature Gallery. In 1850, Brady published the *Gallery of Illustrious Americans,* a portfolio containing 12 lithographs from daguerreotype portraits of contemporary personalities. It became his mission to capture, for posterity, the images of all the prominent figures of his time, which led to the opening of a second studio in Washington, D.C. The *Daily National Intelligencer,* a Washington paper, wrote early in 1849 that Brady had arrived "for the purpose of obtaining daguerreotype portraits of all the distinguished men who may be present at the approaching Inauguration" (Panzer, p. xv). Although this studio did not last, Brady returned to Washington, D.C. in 1858 to open a successful gallery on Pennsylvania Avenue, managed by Alexander Gardner.

Brady had both tremendous success and failure throughout his fifty years in the photography business. He was at all times his own best promoter. An advertisement in the Horblit collection, clipped from the pages of an 1853 journal, reads, "Brady's daguerreotypes were awarded at the World's Fair, in London, 1851, the prize medal, for the best daguerreotypes in New York. Brady's Daguerreotypes have invariably commanded the highest prizes whenever offered for competition. The proprietor has no hesitation in claiming for his new Gallery, 359 Broadway, advantages possessed by no similar establishment either in this country or in Europe."

R42

Charles DeForest Fredricks, 1823–1894

Postmortem Portrait of a Woman, 1856–1858

Quarter plate daguerreotype

Charles DeForest Fredricks was a celebrated photographer in the United States as well as in South America. At the age of twenty, he learned to make daguerreotypes from Jeremiah Gurney, before traveling to Venezuela. According to Beaumont Newhall, Fredricks was able to get his equipment through customs only by promising to make a postmortem photograph of a wealthy merchant's son. He traveled along the Orinoco and Amazon Rivers, selling and bartering daguerreotypes, and did not return to the United States for ten years. The Horblit collection contains three daguerreotypes with mats stamped, "C. D. Fredricks, 585 Broadway," which was the address of the studio Fredricks maintained in New York City between 1856 and 1858. The sign above his Broadway door read "Photographic Temple of Art." Concurrently, he operated a Cuban affiliate, C. D. Fredricks y Daries.

There are nine postmortem daguerreotypes in the Horblit collection. Photography was commonly used in the nineteenth century to memorialize the dead, particularly young children, who were often posed in a parent's lap. This image shows a young woman in her coffin with a decorative, paisley drape covering all but her head and neck. In his 1855 article, "Taking Portraits after Death," Fredricks's partner, Nathan G. Burgess, recommends, "Should the body be in the coffin, it still can be taken, though not quite so conveniently, nor with so good results. . . . It is of considerable importance that the coffin should not appear in the picture, and it may be covered around the edges by means of a piece of colored cloth, a shawl, or any drapery that will conceal it from view" (Burgess, p. 80). The cheeks and lips are hand-colored, as in most portrait daguerreotypes.

R43

Frederick Langenheim, 1809–1879, and William Langenheim, 1807–1874
Portrait of Seated Man Holding a Walking Stick

Half plate daguerreotype

Marcus Aurelius Root, a daguerreotypist and the first biographer of American photographers, wrote, "in 1845–6, F. Langenheim . . . was generally acknowledged to be the first scientific and practical daguerreotypist in this country, and probably in the world." (Root, p. 363.) Frederick's older brother, William, practiced law before leaving Germany for Texas in 1834. Frederick joined him in Philadelphia around 1840, where the brothers opened a daguerreotype studio—William handled the books, and Frederick the camera. They received a certificate of honorable mention for their work in the 1843 exhibition of the Franklin Institute and, in the 1845 show, took the medal away from the leading daguerreotypist of the day, John Plumbe, Jr. This was also the year they received international acclaim for their eight daguerreotype panorama of Niagara Falls. At least eight complete sets of the panorama were produced and sent to heads of state around the world, as well as Daguerre himself. Honors and awards came back from Queen Victoria, President Polk, and others, including a medal mentioned in the *Philadelphia Public Ledger:* "Valuable Present.—Messrs. Langenheim, the eminent Daguerreotypist, a few days since received, through the Consul General of Wurtemberg, residing in Baltimore, a handsome gold medal, in return for a set of plates containing the views of Niagara, taken on the spot during the last year, and transmitted some months since to the King of Wurtemberg" (May 7, 1846). The brothers still had no money, but their reputation was ensured.

The Langenheims always made use of the latest technological innovations. Their early daguerreotypes were round, made with a conical, all-metal camera made by Peter Friedrich Voigtländer and a newly designed portrait lens by Josef Petzval. They experimented with all types of photographic formats, including talbotypes, hyalotypes (a modified albumen-on-glass process based on Niepce de Saint Victor's formula), and stereoscopic views on both glass and paper. Their studio continued until the death of William in 1874, at which time Frederick sold the business to their main competitor, Dr. Casper Briggs.

R44

Photographer unknown

Portrait of Robert Peel, 1852

Whole plate daguerreotype

A note accompanying this daguerreotype identifies it as a portrait of "Robert Peel, at the age of 10 years & 17 weeks, taken 14 Sept. 1852. The day on which he first went to school & the day on which the great Duke of Wellington died."

R45

American School

Portrait of Graduating Class of Rutgers Female Institute, ca. 1853

Half plate daguerreotype

The Rutgers Female Institute was located at Fifth Avenue and 42nd Street in New York City, the present site of the New York Public Library's Humanities Research Division. The institute was one of the most liberal schools for woman at the time and was also progressive in its use of photography to document the graduating class. In her book, *First Photographs,* Gail Buckland describes a daguerreotype (11 x 14") of the institute's 1851 graduating class, which she believed to be one of the earliest class portraits of this kind. The Horblit collection also includes a portrait of an all-male graduating class created from thirty individual portraits re-daguerreotyped to form a single image (see R46). Beginning in the early 1840s both Harvard and Yale used photography to memorialize graduating classes. Also in the Horblit collection is a Harvard class album entitled *Harvard College Photographs. Class of Sixty-Nine,* which contains 160 albumen portraits of students and faculty and 31 campus views. Similar Harvard photographs have been attributed to John Whipple, who was active in Boston at the time.

R46

American School

Portraits of Thirty Men, Copy Daguerreotype of Graduating Class

Whole plate daguerreotype

R47

American School

Portrait of a Seated Man and a Standing Woman Holding a Fan

Quarter plate daguerreotype

CATALOGUE NO. R45. American School. *Portrait of Graduating Class of Rutgers Female Institute,* ca. 1853. Half plate daguerreotype

R48

American School

Portrait of a Woman

Sixteenth plate daguerreotype

R49

American School

Portrait of a Boy Wearing a Military Uniform, Standing beside a Chair

Half plate daguerreotype

R50

American School

Portrait of a Man, a Woman, and Two Girls in Exterior Setting

Quarter plate daguerreotype

R51

American School

Portrait of a Seated Man with His Arm around a Standing Girl

Whole plate daguerreotype

R52

American School

Portrait of a Woman Seated in an Ornate Chair

Mammoth plate daguerreotype

CATALOGUE NO. R47. American School. *Portrait of a Seated Man and a Standing Woman Holding a Fan.* Quarter plate daguerreotype

Also on view

F. A. Wenderoth, 1814–1884 (attributed to)
Portrait of Unknown Gentleman, 1870s
Mammoth ivorytype, hand-painted and matted, in contemporary frame

F. A. Wenderoth, 1814–1884 (attributed to)
Portrait of Unknown Woman, 1870s
Mammoth ivorytype, hand-painted and matted, in contemporary frame

American School
Nine Framed Portraits, 1880s–1890s
Tintypes in wooden frame

Lucius O. Churchill (attributed to)
City and Harbor of Gloucester, Massachusetts, 1870s–1880s
Albumen silver print; image: 32.1 x 56.5 cm., mount: 53.3 x 78.1 cm.

American School
Portrait of Three Women, Three Boys, and a Man Holding a Baby
Whole plate daguerreotype set in the cover of a sewing box

Egyptian School
Construction of the Suez Canal, 1860s
Four bromide prints forming a panorama; image: 20 x 104.5 cm., mount: 46 x 114.6 cm.

Wilhelm Hammerschmidt, died 1869
Panorama de Jerusalem, vue du mont des Oliviers, 1870s
Four albumen silver prints forming a panorama; image: 21.6 x 106.7 cm., mount: 32.1 x 116.8 cm.

French wet plate view camera
Wooden folding camera with leather bellows, brass Berthiot lens, plate holders, carrying case, and lens bag: 40 x 55 x 17 cm.

European wet plate studio camera
Wooden folding camera (lens missing) with leather bellows, film holders, and printing frame: 32 x 56 x 9.5 cm.

BIBLIOGRAPHY

Albums photographiques édités par Blanquart-Evrard, 1851–1855. Paris: Kodak-Pathé, 1878.

Annan, Thomas. *Photographs of the Old Closes and Streets of Glasgow 1868–1877,* with a New Introduction by Anita Ventura Mozley. New York: Dover, 1977.

Apraxine, Pierre. *Photographs from the Collection of the Gilman Paper Company.* United States: White Oak Press, 1985.

Armstrong, Carol. "Julia Margaret Cameron and the Maternalization of Photography." *October* 76 (Spring 1996): 115–41.

Arnold, H. J. P. *William Henry Fox Talbot.* London: Hutchinson Benham, 1977.

The Art-Journal Illustrated Catalogue: The Industry of All Nations 1851. London: George Virtue, 1851.

Auer, Michèle, and Michel Auer. *Encyclopédie internationale des photographes de 1839 à nos jours.* Hermance, Switzerland: Editions Camera Obscura, 1985.

Baedeker, Karl. *Central Italy and Rome: Handbook for Travellers.* New York: Charles Scribner's Sons, 1909.

Baker, Paul R. *Richard Morris Hunt.* Cambridge, Mass.: MIT Press, 1980.

Baldwin, Gordon. *Roger Fenton: Pasha and Bayadere.* Malibu, Calif. : J. Paul Getty Museum, 1996.

Bannon, Anthony. *The Taking of Niagara: A History of the Falls in Photography.* Buffalo, N.Y.: Media Study, 1982.

Banta, Melissa, and Curtis M. Hinsley. *From Site to Sight.* Cambridge, Mass.: Peabody Museum, 1986.

Baty, Laurie A. *"Proud of the Result of My Labor,* Frederick DeBourg Richards (1822–1903)." Daguerreian Society Annual (1995): 207–25.

Becchetti, Piero. *Fotografi e fotografia in Italia, 1839–1880.* Roma: Quasar, 1978.

———. *Roma nelle fotografie dei fratelli D'Alessandri, 1858–1930.* Prezentazione di Oreste Ferrari. Roma: Editore Colombo, 1996.

Beeley, Serena. *A History of Bicycles.* London: Studio Editions, 1992.

Berg, Paul K. *19th-Century Photographic Cases and Wall Frames.* Huntington Beach, Calif.: Huntington Valley Press, 1995.

Berger, Janet E. "Daguerre." *Image* 28, no. 2 (June 1985): 2–20.

Bonfils, Félix. *Catalogue des vues photographiques de l'Orient, photographiées et éditées par Bonfils.* Alais, A. Brugueirolle, 1876.

———. *Remembrances of the Near East: The Photographs of Bonfils, 1867–1907,* from the Collections of the International Museum of Photography at George Eastman House and the Harvard Semitic Museum. Rochester: International Museum of Photography, 1980.

————. *Souvenirs d'Orient. Album pittoresque des sites, villes et ruines les plus remarquables de l'Egypte et de la Nubie (de la Palestine, de la Syrie et de la Grèce),* avec notice en regard de chaque planche. Alais: Chez l'auteur, 1878. 5 vols.

Borcoman, James. *Magicians of Light.* Ottawa: National Gallery of Canada, 1993.

Brettell, Richard R. *Paper and Light: The Calotype in France and Great Britain, 1839–1870.* Boston: David R. Godine, 1984.

Brey, William, "The Langenheims of Philadelphia." *Stereo World* 6, no. 1 (March–April 1979): 4–20.

Browne, Turner, and Elaine Partnow. *Macmillan Biographical Encyclopedia of Photographic Artists & Innovators.* New York: Macmillan, 1983.

Buckland, Gail. *First Photographs: People, Places, and Phenomena as Captured for the First Time by the Camera.* New York: Macmillan, 1980.

————. *Fox Talbot and the Invention of Photography.* Boston: David R. Godine, 1980.

Buckman, Rollin. *The Photographic Work of Calvert Richard Jones.* London: Science Museum, 1990.

Burke, Bernard, Sir. *A Genealogical and Heraldic History of the Landed Gentry of Great Britain & Ireland.* London: Burke's Peerage, 1850–1926.

Burgess, N. G. "Taking Portraits after Death." *Photographic and Fine Art Journal* 8, no. 3 (March 1855): 80.

Burns, Stanley B. *Early Medical Photography in America (1839–1883).* New York: The Burns Archive, 1983. 5 pts. in 1 vol.

————. *Forgotten Marriage: The Painted Tintype & the Decorative Frame 1860–1910.* New York: Burns Collection, 1995.

"The Calotype Society." *Athenaeum* 1054 (December 18, 1847): 1304.

Cameron, Julia Margaret Pattle. *Annals of My Glass House.* Unfinished manuscript first published in the Cameron exhibition catalogue for the Camera Gallery, London (April 1889), reprinted in Helmut Gernsheim. *Julia Margaret Cameron: Her Life and Photographic Work.* Millerton, N.Y.: Aperture, 1975.

Carroll, Roger. *Lebanon 1761–1994: The Evolution of a Resilient New Hampshire City.* West Kennebunk, Maine: Phoenix Publishing, 1994.

Chappell, Walter. "Robertson Beato & Co.: Camera Vision at Lucknow, 1857–58." *Image* 7, no. 2 (February 1958): 35–40.

Charcot, J. M. *Oeuvres complètes.* Paris: Lecrosnier et Babé, 1888–1894. 9 vols.

Çizgen, Engin. *Photography in the Ottoman Empire 1839–1919.* Istanbul: Ha et Kitabevi, 1987.

————. *Photography in Turkey (1842–1936).* [Turkey: s.n., 1981].

Cobb, Josephine. "Alexander Gardner." *Image* 7, no. 6 (June 1958): 124–36.

Coe, Brian. *Cameras: From Daguerreotypes to Instant Pictures.* New York: Crown Publishers, 1978.

Cohen, Morton N. *Lewis Carroll: A Biography.* London: Macmillan, 1995.

Coke, Van Deren. "Georgio Sommer." *The Bulletin of the University of New Mexico,* no. 9 (1975–76): 22–24.

Couling, David. *An Isle of Wight Camera 1856–1914.* Wimborne, England: Dovecote Press, 1978.

Cox, Julian. "Photography in South Wales 1840–60: *This Beautiful Art.*" *History of Photography* 15, no. 3 (Autumn 1991): 160–70.

Craig's Daguerreian Registry. http://www.daguerreotype.com

The Crystal Palace Exhibition Illustrated Catalogue, London 1851. Reprint. New York: Dover Publications, 1970.

The Crystal Palace: Photographs by Philip H. Delamotte. Rochester, N.Y.: International Museum of Photography at George Eastman House, 1980.

Daguerreian Annual. Eureka, Calif.: Daguerreian Society, 1990–1997.

Darrah, William Culp. *Cartes de Visite in Nineteenth-Century Photography.* Gettysburg, Pa.: Darrah, 1981.

———. *The World of Stereographs.* Gettysburg, Pa.: Darrah, 1977.

Darwin, Charles. *The Expression of the Emotions in Man and Animals, with Photographic and Other Illustrations.* London: John Murray, 1872.

Darwin, Francis. *The Life and Letters of Charles Darwin.* New York: D. Appleton, 1911.

Date, Christopher, and Anthony Hamber. "The Origins of Photography at the British Museum, 1839–1860." *History of Photography* 14, no. 4 (October–December 1990): 309–25.

De Angeli, Stefano. *Templum Divi Vespasiani.* Roma: De Luca Edizione d'Arte, 1992.

Didi-Huberman, Georges. *Invention de l'hystérie: Charcot et l'iconographie photographique de la Salpêtrière.* Paris: Macula, 1982.

Dimond, Frances, and Roger Taylor. *Crown & Camera: the Royal Family and Photography, 1842–1910.* New York: Penguin, 1987.

A Directory of Massachusetts Photographers 1839–1900. Research by Chris Steele and Ronald Polito. Edited by Ronald Polito. Camden, Maine: Picton Press, 1993.

Dodgson, Charles Lutwidge. Directions regarding my funeral &c. Autograph manuscript, June 4, 1873, p. 4. BMS Eng 718.11 (5). The Houghton Library, Harvard University.

Du Camp, Maxime. *Literary Recollections.* 2 vols. London: Remington & Co., 1893.

Emerson, Peter Henry. *Naturalistic Photography for Students of the Art.* Facsimile ed. New York: Arno Press, 1973.

———. *P. H. Emerson, Photographer of Norfolk.* [Text by] Peter Turner and Richard Wood. London: Gordon Fraser Gallery, 1974.

En Égypte au temps de Flaubert: 1839–1860, les premiers photographes [exposition conçue par Marie-Thérèse et André Jammes], 2e édition. Paris: Kodak-Pathé, [1980].

Encyclopaedia Judaica. Jerusalem: Keter Publishing House, 1971.

Erlande-Brandenburg, Alain. *Notre-Dame de Paris.* Photographs by Caroline Rose. New York: Harry N. Abrams, 1998.

Excursions Along the Nile: The Photographic Discovery of Ancient Egypt. Essay by Kathleen Stewart Howe. Santa Barbara, Calif.: Santa Barbara Museum of Art, 1993.

Falconer, John. "The Photograph Collection of the Royal Commonwealth Society." *The Photograph Collector* 2, no. 1 (Spring 1981): 34–39.

Fenton, Roger. "Narrative of a Photographic Trip to the Seat of War in the Crimea." *The Journal of the Photographic Society* no. 38 (January 21, 1856): 284–91.

The Ferrotyper's Guide: A Complete Manual of Instruction in the Art of Ferrotyping. New York: Scovill Manufacturing Company, 1873.

Field, Henry M. *Gibraltar.* New York: Charles Scribner's Sons, 1888.

Finkel, Kenneth. *Nineteenth-Century Photography in Philadelphia.* New York: Dover Publications in cooperation with the Library Company of Philadelphia, 1980.

Fisher, A. L. "Thomas Annan's *Old Closes and Streets of Glasgow* (Part I)." *Scottish Photography Bulletin* (Spring 1987): 4–8.

———. "Thomas Annan's *Old Closes and Streets of Glasgow:* A Catalogue of the Images." *Scottish Photography Bulletin* (Autumn 1987): 2–13.

Flaubert, Gustave. *Flaubert in Egypt, a Sensibility on Tour: A Narrative Drawing from Gustave Flaubert's Travel Notes & Letters,* tr. and ed. by Francis Steegmuller. Chicago: Academy Chicago Ltd., 1979.

Fostle, D. W. *The Steinway Saga.* New York: Scribner, 1995.

Freeman, J. E. *Gatherings from an Artist's Portfolio.* New York: D. Appleton, 1877–1883.

Freeman, Ray. *Dartmouth: A New History of the Port and Its People.* Dartmouth, England: Harbour Books, 1983.

Freeman, Richard Broke. *The Works of Charles Darwin: An Annotated Bibliographical Handlist.* 2nd ed. Hamden, Conn.: Archon Books, 1977.

Frith, Francis. *Egypt and the Holy Land in Historic Photographs: 77 Views by Francis Frith.* Introduction and bibliography by Julia Van Haaften, selection and commentary by John E. Manchip White. New York: Dover Publications, 1980.

Garnett, Lucy M. J. *Mysticism and Magic in Turkey.* London: Pitman & Sons, Ltd., 1912.

Gavin, Carney E. S. "Bonfils and the Early Photography of the Near East." *Harvard Library Bulletin* XXV, no. 4 (October 1978): 442–70.

Gavin, Carney E. S. *The Image of the East: Nineteenth-Century Near Eastern Photographs by Bonfils from the Collections of the Harvard Semitic Museum.* Compiled and edited by Ingeborg Endter O'Reilly. Chicago: University of Chicago Press, 1982.

Gernsheim, Helmut. *The History of Photography from the Camera Obscura to the Beginning of the Modern Era.* Rev. ed. London: Thames and Hudson, 1969.

————. *Incunabula of British Photographic Literature, 1839–1875.* London and Berkeley: Scholar Press, 1984.

————. *Lewis Carroll: Photographer.* Rev. ed. New York: Dover, 1969.

————. *Roger Fenton: Photographer of the Crimean War.* London: Secker & Warburg, 1954.

————. "The World's First Photographic Manual and the English Editions of Daguerre's Manuals." *Photographic Journal,* XC, Section A (September 1950): 308–10.

Giorgio Sommer fotografo a Napoli. Curated by Daniela Palazzoli. Milan: Electa, 1981.

Gleason, Herbert W. *Through the Year with Thoreau: Sketches from Nature from the Writings of Henry D. Thoreau, with Corresponding Photographic Illustrations.* Boston: Houghton Mifflin, 1917.

Goldschmidt, Lucien, and Weston Naef. *The Truthful Lens: A Survey of the Photographically Illustrated Book, 1844–1914.* New York: Grolier Club, 1980.

González, Juan Carlos Pardo. "El Gibraltar de 1851–52 en los Calotipos de Alfred Capel Cure." *Jornadas de Historia del Campo de Gibraltar* 4, número 17 (Abril 1997): 227–47.

Gopnik, Adam. "Wonderland: Lewis Carroll and the Loves of His Life." *The New Yorker* (October 9, 1995): 82–90.

Gutman, Judith Mara. *Through Indian Eyes: 19th and Early 20th Century Photography from India.* New York: Oxford University Press and International Center of Photography, 1982.

Hall, Samuel Carter. *Retrospect of a Long Life: From 1815–1883.* New York: D. Appleton, 1883.

Hamber, Anthony. "The Photography of the Visual Arts, 1839–1880." *Visual Resources* part 1: 5, no. 4 (Winter 1989): 289–310; part 2: 6, no. 1 (1989): 19–41; part 3: 6, no. 2 (1989): 165–79; part 4: 6, no. 3 (1990): 219–41.

Hamdi, Osman, Bey. *Les costumes populaires de la Turquie en 1873.* Ouvrage publié sous le patronage de la Commission Impériale Ottomane pour l'Exposition Universelle de Vienne. Texte par Hamdy Bey et Marie de Launay. Phototypie par Sébah. Constantinople: Imprimerie du "Levant Times & Shipping Gazette," 1873.

Hanson, David A. "The Beginnings of Photographic Reproduction in the USA." *History of Photography* 12, no. 4 (October–December 1988): 357–73.

Hare, Augustus J. C. *Walks in Rome.* 21st ed. by St. Clair Baddeley. London: Kegan Paul, Trench, Trubner, & Company, 1923.

Harker, Margaret. "From Mansion to Close: Thomas Annan, Master Photographer." *The Photographic Collector* 5, no. 1 (1984): 81–95.

Hawarth-Loomes, B. E. C. *Victorian Photography.* London: Ward Lock, 1974.

Hawes, Josiah Johnson. "Stray Leaves from the Diary of the Oldest Professional Photographer in the World." *Photo-Era* 16, no. 2 (February 1906): 104–07.

Hawks, Francis L. *Narrative of the Expedition of an American Squadron to the China Seas and Japan, Performed in the Years 1852, 1853, and 1854, under the Command of Commodore M. C. Perry, United States Navy.* New York: D. Appleton, 1857.

Haworth-Booth, Mark. *Photography: An Independent Art.* Princeton, N.J.: Princeton University Press, 1997.

Haworth-Booth, Mark, and Anne McCauley. *The Museum & the Photograph*. Williamstown, Mass.: Sterling and Francine Clark Art Institute, 1998.

Henisch, Heinz K., and Bridget A. Henisch. "James Robertson of Constantinople." *History of Photography* 8, no. 4 (October–December 1984): 299–313.

———. *The Painted Photograph 1839–1914*. University Park, Pa.: Pennsylvania State University Press, 1996.

———. *The Photographic Experience, 1839–1914*. University Park, Pa.: Pennsylvania State University Press, 1994.

Hobhouse, Christopher. *1851 and the Crystal Palace*. London: John Murray, 1937.

Holland, Patricia. "Sweet It Is to Scan . . . : Personal Photographs and Popular Photography." In *Photography: A Critical Introduction*. Liz Wells, ed. London: Routledge, 1997.

Homer, Rachel Johnston, ed. *The Legacy of Josiah Johnson Hawes: 19th Century Photographs of Boston*. Barre, Mass.: Barre Publishers, 1972.

Horblit, Harrison D. *One Hundred Books Famous in Science: Based on an Exhibition Held at the Grolier Club*. New York: Grolier Club, 1964.

Howard, James Murray. "Richard Morris Hunt: The Development of His Stylistic Attitudes." Ph.D. dissertation, University of Illinois at Urbana-Champaign, 1982.

How to Colour a Photograph; or, Lessons on the Harmony and Contrast of Colours, Principally in Their Application to Photography. Reprinted from the *Photographic News*. London: Cassell, Petter, and Galpin, 1859.

Hudson, Derek. *Holland House in Kensington*. London: Peter Davies, 1967.

Hunt, Robert. *A Popular Treatise on the Art of Photography*. A facsimile edition with introduction and notes by James Yingpeh Tong. Athens: Ohio University Press, 1973.

Index to American Photographic Collections, George Eastman database. Telnet address: geh.org

In Focus: Julia Margaret Cameron: Photographs from the J. Paul Getty Museum. Santa Monica, Calif.: J. Paul Getty Museum, 1995.

The Invention of Photography and Its Impact on Learning: Photographs from Harvard University and Radcliffe College and from the Collection of Harrison D. Horblit. Louise Todd Ambler and Melissa Banta, eds. Cambridge, Mass.: Harvard University Library, 1989.

Jammes, André, and Eugenia Parry Janis. *The Art of French Calotype: With a Critical Dictionary of Photographers*, 1845–1870. Princeton, N.J.: Princeton University Press, 1983.

Jammes, Isabelle. *Blanquart-Evrard et les origines de l'édition photographique française*: Catalogue raisonné des albums photographiques édités 1851–1855. Genève: Librarie Droz, 1981.

Janis, Eugenia Parry. *The Invention of Photography and its Impact on Learning: The Collection of Harrison D. Horblit, A Loan Exhibition at the Houghton Library, Harvard University*. Exhibition brochure. Cambridge, Mass.: Houghton Library, 1989.

———. "The Man on the Tower of Notre Dame: New Light on Henri LeSecq." *Image* 19, no. 4 (December 1976): 13–25.

———. *The Photography of Gustave Le Gray*. Chicago: Art Institute of Chicago, 1987.

Johnson, William. *Nineteenth-Century Photography: An Annotated Bibliography, 1839–1879*. Boston: G. K. Hall, 1990.

Jones, Bernard E., ed. *Encyclopedia of Photography*. New York: Arno Press, 1974.

Jones, Iwan Meical. "Calvert Richard Jones: the Earlier Work." *History of Photography* 15, no. 3 (Autumn 1991): 174–79.

Kahan, Robert S., and J. B. Colson. "Peter Henry Emerson." *The Library Chronicle of the University of Texas at Austin*, New Series (September 1972): 68–81.

Keeler, Nancy B. "Illustrating the *Reports by the Juries* of the Great Exhibition of 1851; Talbot, Henneman, and Their Failed Commission." *History of Photography* 6, no. 3 (July 1982): 257–72.

Kempe, Fritz. *Daguerreotypie in Deutschland: vom Charme der frühen Fotografie*. Seebruck am Chiemsee: Heering-Verlag, 1979.

Kraus, Hans P., Jr. *Sun Pictures*. Research and text by Larry J. Schaaf. New York: Kraus, 1984–1997, no. 1–8.

Layne, George S. "The Langenheims of Philadelphia." *History of Photography* 2, no. 1 (January–March 1987): 39–52.

Levine, Robert M. *Cuba in the 1850s: Through the Lens of Charles DeForest Fredricks*. Tampa, Fla.: University of South Florida Press, 1990.

Linkman, Audrey. *The Victorians: Photographic Portraits*. London: Tauris Parke Books, 1993.

Londe, A. *La photographie médicale: Application aux sciences médicales et physiologiques*. Préface de M. Charcot. Paris: Gauthier-Villars, 1893.

Looney, Robert F. *Old Philadelphia in Early Photographs 1839–1914*. New York: Dover, 1976.

Lothrop, Eaton S. *A Century of Cameras, from the Collection of the International Museum of Photography at George Eastman House*. Dobbs Ferry, N.Y.: Morgan & Morgan, 1973.

Lothrop, Samuel Kirkland. *A History of the Church in Brattle Street, Boston*. Boston: William Crosby and H.P. Nichols, 1851.

Lowry, Bates, and Isabel Barret Lowry. *The Silver Canvas: Daguerreotype Masterpieces from the J. Paul Getty Museum*. Los Angeles: J. Paul Getty Museum, 1998.

Luigi Canina (1795–1856): Architetti e Teorico del Classicismo, a cura di Augusto Sistri, prefazione di Werner Oechslin. Milano: Guerini e associati, 1995.

Marville, Charles. *Charles Marville, Photographs of Paris at the Time of the Second Empire*, on loan from the Musée Carnavalet. [Exhibition] Catalogue edited and designed by Jacqueline Chambord. New York: French Institute/Alliance Française, 1981.

The Massachusetts Register. Boston: George Adams, 1853.

McCauley, Elizabeth Anne. *Industrial Madness: Commercial Photography in Paris, 1848–1871*. New Haven: Yale University, 1994.

McCosh, J. *Advice to Officers in India*. Cited in Gary David Sampson. "Samuel Bourne and 19th-Century British Landscape Photography in India." Ph.D. dissertation, University of California, Santa Barbara, 1991.

McGurn, James. *On Your Bicycle*. New York: Facts on File Publications, 1987.

McKenzie, Ray. "The Cradle and Grave of Empires: Robert Macpherson and the Photography of Nineteenth Century Rome." *The Photographic Collector* 4, no. 2 (Autumn 1983): 215–34.

———. "The Noble Shape of a Long-Decaying Corpse: Robert Macpherson and the Photography of Nineteenth Century Rome." *Scotland & Italy: Papers Presented at the Fourth Annual Conference of the Scottish Society for Art History*. Edinburgh: Scottish Society for Art History, [1990?]

Miller, Frances. *Catalogue of the William James Stillman Collection*. Schenectady, N.Y.: Friends of the Union College Library, 1974.

Miraglia, Marina. "Giorgio Sommer's Italian Journey: Between Tradition and the Popular Image." *History of Photography* 20, no. 1 (Spring 1996): 41–48.

Moffat, John. *John Moffat, Pioneer Scottish Photographic Artist 1819–1894*. Eastbourne, England: J. S. M. Publishing, 198?.

Morris, Richard. *John Dillwyn Llewelyn 1810–1822* [sic]. [Cardiff, Wales]: Welsh Arts Council, 1980.

Morton, Vanda. *Oxford Rebels: The Life and Friends of Nevil Story Maskelyne 1823–1911*. Gloucester, England: Alan Sutton, 1987

Munsterberg, Marjorie. "A Biographical Sketch of Robert Macpherson." *Art Bulletin* 68, no. 1 (March 1986): 142–53.

Murray, John. *A Handbook for Travellers in Central Italy. Part II: Rome and its Environs*. 4th ed., rev. London: Murray, 1856.

Mushkat, Jerome. *Tammany: The Evolution of a Political Machine 1789–1865*. Syracuse, N.Y.: Syracuse University Press, 1971.

Naef, Weston. *The J. Paul Getty Museum Handbook of the Photographs Collection*. Malibu, Calif.: J. Paul Getty Museum, 1995.

Negretti, P. A. "Henry Negretti: Gentleman and Photographic Pioneer." *The Photographic Collector* 5, no. 1 (1984): 96–105.

Newhall, Beaumont. "A Chronicle of the Birth of Photography." *Harvard Library Bulletin* VII (1953): 208–19.

———. *The Daguerreotype in America*. 3rd ed., rev. New York: Dover, 1976.

Newhall, Nancy Wynne. *P. H. Emerson: The Fight for Photography as a Fine Art*. New York: Aperture, 1975.

Ochsner, Jeffrey Karl. *H. H. Richardson: Complete Architectural Works*. Cambridge, Mass.: MIT Press, 1982.

Osman, Collin. "Antonio Beato, Photographer of the Nile." *History of Photography* 14, no. 2 (April–June 1990): 101–11.

———. "The Later Years of James Robertson." *History of Photography* 16, no. 1 (Spring 1992): 72–73.

Painting, David. "J. D. Llewelyn and His Family Circle." *History of Photography* 15, no. 3 (Autumn 1991): 180–85.

Palmquist, Peter E. "Raffle Wars: A Chronology of Alphonse J. Liébert in California and France." *Daguerreian Annual* 1992: 144–63.

Panzer, Mary. *Mathew Brady and the Image of History*. Washington, D.C.: Smithsonian Institution, 1997.

Pare, Richard. *Photography and Architecture: 1839–1939*. Montreal: Centre Canadien d'Architecture, 1982.

Peterich, Gerda. "Photography at the Great Exhibition 1851." *Image* 7, no. 3 (March 1958): 53–58.

Philipp, Claudia Gabriele, Dietmar Siegert, and Rainer Wick. *Felice Beato: Viaggio in Giappone 1863–1877*. Milan: Federico Motta Editore, 1991.

Philobiblon Society (Great Britain). "Edward Cheney, in Memoriam." *Miscellanies of the Philobiblon Society* 15 (1877–84): 1–18.

Photography: the First Eighty Years. London: P. & D. Colnaghi & Co., 1976.

Pierce, Sally. *Whipple and Black: Commercial Photographers in Boston*. Boston: Boston Athenaeum, 1987.

Pittori fotografi a Roma 1845–1870. Roma: Multigrafica, 1987.

Reynolds, Léonie L., and Arthur T. Gill. "The Mayall Story." *History of Photography* 9, no. 2 (April–June 1985): 89–107.

Rinhart, Floyd, and Marion Rinhart. *The American Daguerreotype*. Athens, Ga.: University of Georgia Press, 1981.

Roberts, Helene E. *British Art Periodicals of the Eighteenth and Nineteenth Centuries*. Bloomington, Ind.: Research Society of Victorian Periodicals, 1970.

Rome in Early Photographs: The Age of Pius IX. Translated by Ann Thornton. Copenhagen: The Thorvaldsen Museum, 1977.

Root, Marcus Aurelius. *The Camera and the Pencil*. Pawlet, Vt.: Helios, 1970.

Rudisill, Richard. *Mirror Image: The Influence of the Daguerreotype on American Society*. Albuquerque, N.M.: University of New Mexico Press, 1971.

Schaaf, Larry J. *Out of the Shadows: Herschel, Talbot & the Invention of Photography*. New Haven, Conn.: Yale University Press, 1992.

Seiberling, Grace. *Amateurs, Photography, and the Mid-Victorian Imagination*. Chicago: University of Chicago Press, 1986.

Sicard, Monique, Robert Pujade, and Daniel Wallach. *À corps et à raison, photographie médicales 1840–1920*. Paris: Marval, 1995.

Sobieszek, Robert A., and Odette M. Appel. *The Spirit of Fact: The Daguerreotypes of Southworth & Hawes, 1843–1862.* Boston: David R. Godine, 1976.

Strange, Maren. *Symbols of Ideal Life: Social Documentary Photography in America, 1890–1950.* New York: Cambridge University Press, 1989.

Stillman, William James. *The Autobiography of a Journalist.* London: Grant Richards, 1901.

———. *Poetic Localities: Photographs of Adirondacks, Cambridge, Crete, Italy, Athens.* New York: Aperture, 1988.

Stroebel, Leslie, and Richard Zakia, eds. *The Focal Encyclopedia of Photography.* 3rd. ed. Boston: Focal Press, 1993.

Taft, Robert. *Photography and the American Scene: A Social History 1839–1889.* New York: Macmillan, 1942.

Tallis's History and Description of the Crystal Palace and the Exhibition of the World's Industry in 1851. London: John Tallis, [1852].

Teynard, Félix. *Félix Teynard, Calotypes of Egypt: A Catalogue Raisonné.* Essay by Kathleen Stewart Howe; Edited by H. P. Kraus, Jr. New York: H. P. Kraus, Jr., 1992.

Thézy, Marie de. *Marville, Paris,* en collaboration avec Roxane Debuisson. Paris: Hazan, 1994.

Thomas, Ann. *Beauty of Another Order: Photography in Science.* New Haven, Conn.: Yale University Press in association with the National Gallery of Canada, Ottawa, 1997.

Thomas, G. *History of Photography, India, 1840–1980.* Hyderabad, India: Andhra Pradesh State Akademi of Photography, 1981.

———. "Indian Mutiny Veterans: The Tytlers." *History of Photography* 9, no. 4 (October–December 1985): 267–73.

Thomas, Ritchie. "Bonfils & Son, Egypt, Greece and the Levant, 1867–1894." *History of Photography* 3, no. 1 (January 1979): 33–46.

Thoreau, Henry D. *The Illustrated Walden with Photographs from the Gleason Collection.* Text edited by J. Lyndon Shanley. Princeton, N.J.: Princeton University Press, 1973.

Trager, James. *Park Avenue: Street of Dreams.* New York: Athenaeum, 1990.

The Traveller's Hand-Book for Gibraltar with Observations on the Surrounding Country by an Old Inhabitant. London: Cowie, Jolland, 1844.

Tytler, Harriet. *An Englishwoman in India: The Memoirs of Harriet Tytler, 1828–1858.* Anthony Sattin, ed. Oxford: Oxford University Press, 1986.

Van Haaften, Julia. "Original Sun Pictures: A Check List of the New York Public Library's Holdings of Early Works Illustrated with Photographs, 1844–1900." *Bulletin of the New York Public Library* 80 (Spring 1977): 355–415.

Vanderwarker, Peter. *Boston Then & Now.* New York: Dover, 1982.

Vendôme, Hôtel des Ventes. *Photographies anciennes, Succession Comte Frédéric Flacheron* [Auction Sales Catalogue]. Vendôme: 22 March 1987.

Vercoutter, Jean. *L'Egypte à la chambre noire: Francis Frith, photographe de l'Egypte retrouvée.* Paris: Gallimard, 1992.

Ward, John, and Sara Stevenson. *Printed Light: The Scientific Art of William Henry Fox Talbot and David Octavius Hill with Robert Adamson.* Edinburgh: Scottish National Portrait Gallery, 1986.

Weaver, Mike, ed. *Henry Fox Talbot: Selected Texts and Bibliography.* World Photographers Reference Series, vol. 3. Oxford, England: Clio Press, 1992.

Welling, W. *Photography in America: The Formative Years, 1839–1900.* New York: Crowell, 1878.

Winkel, Margarita. *Souvenirs from Japan: Japanese Photography at the Turn of the Century.* London: Bamboo Publishing, 1991.

Wood, John. *America and the Daguerreotype.* Iowa City: University of Iowa Press, 1991.

———. *The Photographic Arts.* Iowa City: University of Iowa Press, 1997.

Wood, R. D. *The Calotype Patent Lawsuit of Talbot v. Laroche 1854.* Bromley, England: R. D. Wood, 1975.

Zannier, Italo. *Le grand tour.* Venice: Canal & Stamperia, 1997.

INDEX

Numbers refer to catalogue entries.